THE
BRANCH MANAGER'S
MANUAL

Written by
BEATRICE JUDELLE

with direction by
CHARLES A. BINDER

Published by
THE
OPERATIONS
DIVISION

NATIONAL RETAIL MERCHANTS ASSOCIATION
100 W. 31st Street, New York, N. Y. 10001

PRINTED IN THE UNITED STATES OF AMERICA
VAN REES PRESS • NEW YORK

FOREWORD

The manager of a branch store occupies a position unique in the present-day department store world. In this era of specialization, he is a generalist—almost a throwback to those all-around merchants of another age who founded our great stores.

Whether his unit is a tiny offshoot of a towering parent or one so nearly autonomous that it merits the title of sister store, the branch manager has problems and opportunities quite different from those of other executives within his own organization.

Recognizing the need of branch executives for a forum in which they could exchange experience among themselves, NRMA in 1965 established its Branch Store Institute seminars under the direction of Robert L. Gur-Arie. The Institute's seminars, in turn, made clear the need for a book of this kind, aimed squarely at the branch manager's complex job.

Branch managers themselves contributed substance and direction to this undertaking. So did retail top management, the NRMA staff, and many interested outsiders. The Association sponsored the project and entrusted the research and writing to Beatrice Judelle, contributing editor to STORES, whose keen interest in branch developments goes back to even before 1952, when she researched and wrote NRMA's very first book on branch stores. Charles A. Binder, vice president and manager, NRMA Operations Division, who has personally experienced the problems and rewards of branch management, brought an insider's view to the supervision and editing of the present work.

To all who made their ideas and experience available, may I express my personal as well as my official thanks. All owners and managers of branch stores, present and future, are greatly in your debt.

JAMES J. BLISS
Executive Vice-President
National Retail Merchants Association

PREFACE

The purpose of this book can be simply stated: To help equip present and future branch managers to function effectively by providing them with a background in all the phases of retailing that are part of their many-faceted jobs. Included are such branch problems as community relations, relations with the shopping center, working with merchandising and promotion staffs, minimizing shortages, and many others. Omitted are matters that are not the direct concern of the branch manager, such as finance and accounting, and those in which he is rarely consulted, such as site selection and the decision to own or rent a branch building.

The procedure followed in working on this manual was first to ask retail top management and branch managers themselves to recommend points to be covered in the light of the responsibilities assumed by heads of branch. Thus given direction, the next step was to locate what was wanted and present it here.

Sources used included:

• Top management of NRMA member stores, reached through the medium of a mail survey;

• Managers of branch stores, reached through the medium of a survey and also through individual interviews before and after the survey was made;

• Vice-presidents in charge of branch stores, contacted individually through mail and interview;

• Members of the NRMA staff, who made their reference files, their experience, and their own sound thinking available freely;

• Speakers and participants at the NRMA's seminars for branch store managers;

• Speakers at convention sessions of NRMA and its various divisions and groups;

• STORES Magazine;

• Outside specialists in fields touching upon branch management—architecture, protection, shopping center management, executive techniques, among others.

A special note of appreciation is extended to Janet Cinquemani of the NRMA Operations Division's staff for her assistance in preparing the many forms and charts included in this book.

To enumerate the contributions of all the busy and competent people who participated in this undertaking is almost impossible; the list would be too long. Instead, we offer, in this general and inadequate way, for ourselves and for branch store managers, sincere thanks and a deep sense of obligation.

CHARLES A. BINDER
BEATRICE JUDELLE

CONTENTS

vii

LIST OF EXHIBITS AND FORMS

CHAPTER 1

MANAGEMENT LOOKS AT THE BRANCH

Early in the 1950's, a merchant with an exceptionally clear view of future trends expressed himself on the subject of branch stores. "Our branch," he said, "is our future." He was ahead of his time. His opinion was not then, as it is now, shared by a majority of department specialty store* managements.

In those days, branch volume was only a tiny percentage of a store's total business, and merchants were still debating whether the branch game was worth the candle. To many retailers, it seemed as if an outlying branch would simply transfer part of the downtown store's business to another location. The prospects of adding to total volume substantially via the branch route looked poor. And, indeed, the figures appeared to bear them out. In terms of sales gains, the early branch-owning stores were not much better off than those that ignored the suburbs and concentrated on downtown.

Branches, however, soon began to prove themselves. As suburban living and suburban shopping became increasingly popular, branches contributed a steadily increasing share of total store volume. By 1966, the typical branch-owning organization was getting more than half its volume from its branches. The MOR for 1966 ("Departmental Merchandising and Operating Results," published annually by the Controllers' Congress of NRMA) re-

---

* "Specialty store," as used in this book, refers to any apparel and accessories store that is run along the same general lines as a department store and that, in fact, may be referred to by the public as a department store even though it does not have the full complement of department store departments.

1

ported that branches contributed 52.0 per cent of that year's total sales among department stores, and 47.1 per cent of the total among apparel specialty stores. The percentage has been rising since.

Hold-outs against branches are a rarity today in the department store field. A branch operation, owners say, is necessary for total profit, for giving proper service to customers in outlying areas, for meeting competitive pressures.

Indications of Growth

Branch-owning managements develop a thirst for additional units, once they have lived through the agonies and uncertainties that accompany the first plunge into branch operation.

Branch-owning stores that participated in a survey, made in preparation for this book, offer a case in point. Two in every five of the reporting stores indicated that they expected to open at least one additional branch before the end of the next year. Among these stores, a majority already had four or more branches.

The branches then owned represent a wide range of sizes and locations. Of the reporting stores:

86% had at least one in a suburban shopping center
45% had at least one on a city street
31% had at least one that is less than five miles from the
     main store
30% had at least one that is more than 50 miles from it
24% had at least one free standing branch.

The "twig," or branch that limits its assortment, its departments, or its appeal to a narrow range of customers, is by no means uncommon; one in every four of the reporting stores had at least one. Nearly half (43 per cent) had at least one branch that does less than $2 million a year; one in every eight had at least one that does $20 million or more a year.

Looking ahead, the management spokesmen said they expect branches of the future to be larger and more independent of the parent store than those of today. The small branch, however, does not appear likely to vanish from the picture. Certain localities, particularly those away from the large cities, will continue to need them.

The Branch Manager's Job

The branch manager's job, by all indications, seems destined to grow—in the number and variety of units to be managed, and in the demands upon the managers for initiative and competence. With each new branch that a store adds, the central management has to spread itself so much thinner. Soon the point is reached at which the branches must stand on their own feet for many phases of their work.

Even in organizations with few branches, it is not always expedient to turn constantly to the parent store for service, advice, and decisions. If the branch is large or distant from home base, it will have to settle many of its problems under its own roof. Its manager, like the smaller merchant of another day, will have to be a man of many talents, versed in almost every aspect of retailing.

Unlike the store owner of the past, however, the branch manager does not always have clear-cut authority in all the areas in which he functions. He finds himself in somewhat of an anomalous position.

He is held responsible for volume and profits, yet the bulk of his buying and pricing is done for him by the parent merchandising division. Advertising and promotions are done for him; many displays are planned for him; credit is authorized, supplies are purchased; systems are set up or changed.

He is expected to hire, train, and inspire a staff, yet wage scales and personnel policies are set for him, and much of his staff answers both to him and to executives from the main store. He is expected to watch expenses, yet a large part of the costs charged against his sales are for services performed centrally, beyond his jurisdiction.

Anomaly has its virtues, nonetheless. If electronic data processing is to be adopted, the branch manager has only to learn

SAMPLE ORGANIZATIONAL CHARTS

Example "A"

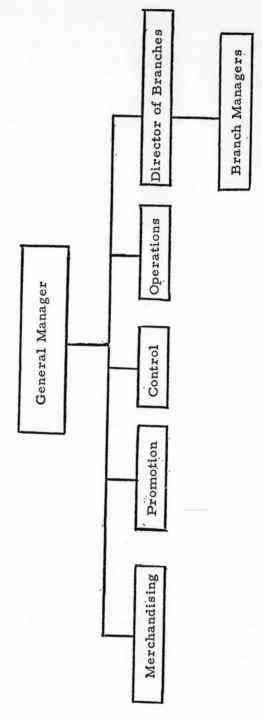

EXHIBIT 1

SAMPLE ORGANIZATIONAL CHARTS

Example "B"

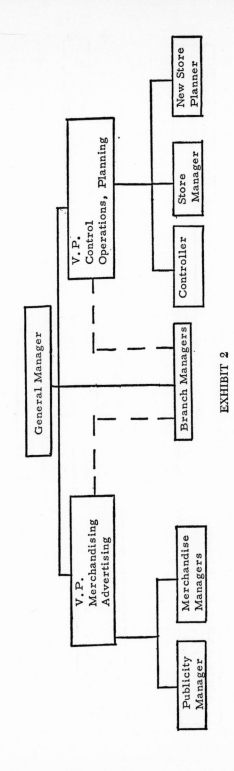

EXHIBIT 2

SAMPLE ORGANIZATIONAL CHARTS

Example "C"

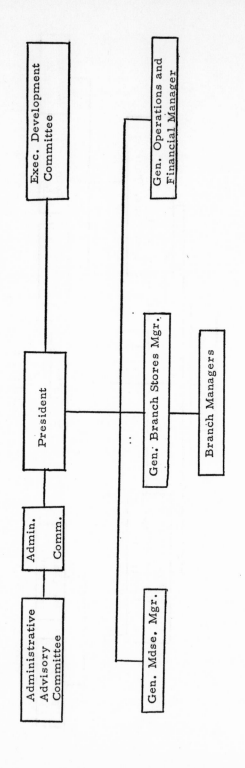

NOTE: General Branch Stores Manager is member of Administrative Committee

and Executive Development Committee.

EXHIBIT 3

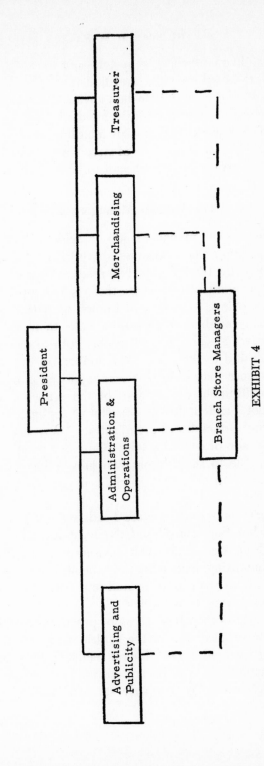

SAMPLE ORGANIZATIONAL CHARTS

Example "D"

President

Advertising and Publicity

Administration & Operations

Merchandising

Treasurer

Branch Store Managers

EXHIBIT 4

how to live with the new system—not to explore, and experiment, make the final decision, and find the money to meet equipment costs. If the market is to be canvassed for types of merchandise or price lines not previously handled, there is a buying staff to do the leg work. If materials handling, or receiving, or security, or any other special phase of store work presents a problem, there is an expert on the parent staff to be consulted.

The Branch Manager's Responsibilities

The branch manager's job is seldom spelled out in detail. Organization charts assume labyrinthine aspects when they seek to blueprint the interlocking relationships of branch and main store personnel. Even where there is a vice-president in charge of branch stores, to whom all branch activities head up, there are still any number of horizontal links to reflect the way branch executives at various levels report both to their higher-ups at the branch and to their opposite numbers at the main store.

No more than half the stores reporting in our survey said they had written-out descriptions of the branch manager's job. This may not, incidentally, be a matter of negligence or of indifference to sound principles of organization. Many store heads may share the opinion of one who said: "Ours is a people business. We like our people to shape their own jobs. What good is a neat little square on an organization chart if you can't find the person to fill it?"

When the reporting store heads were asked, however, to out-line what they considered the most important elements of the branch manager's job, their answers were clear and to the point: Merchandising, leadership, and the ability to maintain good com-munications with his own staff and with the main store. Making a profit, naturally, is implied.

Buying, in the literal sense of procuring merchandise, is essen-tially a responsibility of the central organization, but the branch manager is held responsible for seeing that his unit has the proper merchandise mix for its customers. Store heads want him to see that his branch is "properly stocked" and that its merchandise

BRANCH STORE ORGANIZATION CHARTS

Organization of a Small Branch Store

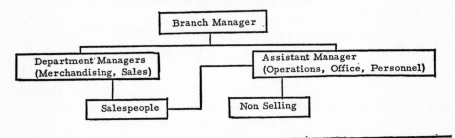

Organization of Medium-Sized Branch Store

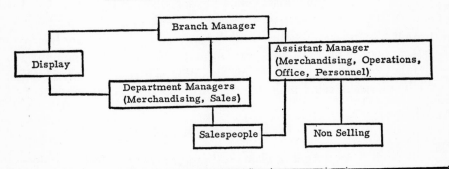

Organization of Larger Branch Store

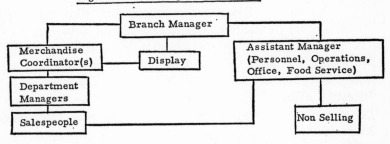

In small branches, assistant manager handles operations while manager supervises merchandising and sales. In medium-sized branches, assistant manager helps branch manager with some of the merchandising responsibilities. In larger branches, merchandise coordinators supervise merchandising.

EXHIBIT 5

is "excitingly" presented, so that sales and profit goals can be achieved.

To accomplish these objectives in an area of shared responsibility and divided authority is not easy. Not surprisingly, management spokesmen want the branch manager to be able to get along well with people and to see that main store and branch personnel work harmoniously together.

He should be a good administrator, too, say heads of stores, with the ability to train and develop an organization at all levels. To maintain morale, to build and motivate a good staff, to teach his people to give the customer service in line with what she expects from the store—all these are his job.

At the same time, management expects him to keep a cool and watchful eye on expense, shrinkage, bad checks, and other items that bite into profits. Responsibilities connected with store housekeeping are also his. So are such intangibles as good community relations and leadership in his shopping center. Few indeed are the phases of retail management with which he is not concerned.

Evaluating the Branch

Profit is important, and many branch managers feel that they are rated solely in terms of the bottom line of the operating statement. The store heads who participated in our survey do look at that bottom line, it is true. But two in every three say they also consider other factors in evaluating branch performance.

Growth was a factor frequently mentioned—not merely growth in the simple sense of increased volume, but growth also in public acceptance, in share of the market, in position in the community. In rating a branch on this point, store heads say they consider the size of the community, any ups and downs in the income of its people, and the nearness and strength of competition.

Managers are rated also by their ability to develop people. The branch manager who surrounds himself with capable people, and who graciously "loses" some of them to bigger jobs in the parent store, can expect to bask in top management approval.

One spokesman for top management rates his branch heads on the basis of how many of their juniors become eligible for buying jobs.

Customer relations are also taken into account. In assessing branch performance, some managements consider the number of customer complaints generated, and the manner in which they have been handled.

Physical appearance of the branch is not overlooked. Since the branch is expected to be a credit to the parent organization and to reflect the image management seeks to create, the housekeeping job is evaluated, along with merchandise presentation and the impression the assortments create upon the customer. In all respects, tangible or otherwise, the branch is rated on its success in creating an atmosphere agreeable to those customers for whom the parent organization plans its merchandising and promotion.

Good morale at the branch is a point in the manager's favor. So is the ability to get along with buyers and merchandise managers at the main store. The smoothness with which he can function in areas of unavoidable divided responsibility is a key measure of the branch manager's competence.

Branch Opportunities

In many senses, the branch manager's job is just what he makes it. Branch heads themselves see it as a composite of merchandising, personnel, liaison, public relations, and a hawk's eye for profit leaks.

They are aware that they must achieve the sales goals set for their units, and they feel that one of their major functions is to keep a smooth flow of merchandise into the branch, to maintain a stock position that meets the demands of their individual trading areas.

Maintaining troop morale, as one branch manager expresses it, is another responsibility that these executives acknowledge as their own. To them, this means finding and training good people and working out the difficult relationship between hours of work and store hours. It means building a staff that not only functions smoothly in its own bailiwick, but that also is capable of cooperation and coordination with the staff of the mother store.

Community relations, customer service, expense control, shortage control, housekeeping, display—all are recognized by branch managers as important elements of their work. Studying the competition, working with other stores in a shopping center, and planning for future growth are also part of the package.

And the incentive for mastering this many-sided job? In many organizations, the branch is the road to recognition. There are reasons for this.

One is the relative smallness of the branch and its staff, in comparison to the ordinary department or specialty store. Young people who are good executive material can show what they can do, with less danger of being lost in the crowd.

In organizations with few branches, top management often regards these as its particular darlings, to be watched over and visited. A splendid showcase for young talent! On the other hand, where there are several branches, comparisons among them are a natural thing. The branch, or the individual department within one, that does a superlative job is quickly spotted.

Then, too, simply because branches exist, the steps up the executive ladder are less extreme and more numerous than they were in the days of huge, single-unit organizations. A promising assistant buyer can move out to the branch as a department manager. A good branch department manager can move back to the main store as a buyer. Supervisors and divisional coordinators, each managing several departments at a branch, can look forward to divisional merchandising jobs in the parent organization.

As for the manager himself: When he has mastered merchandising, personnel, public relations, expense control, and all the many other elements of his job, not forgetting the fine art of functioning in areas of overlapping authority and divided responsibility, isn't he likely to be the stuff of which tomorrow's top management will be made?

CHAPTER 2

LEADERSHIP IN THE BRANCH

The secret ingredient in many a branch store's success is leadership, pure and simple. Stores, we are often told, are not so different from one another in appearance or in merchandise assortments that these differences alone can account for the wide variations in their ability to win customers and achieve profits. It is the people in the organization who make the difference— and the branch manager who makes the people what they are by the leadership he exerts.

Leadership comes instinctively to a few. Most executives, however, have to learn the basic principles of managing people before they hit their full stride in this area. A branch manager, operating within the framework of the parent store's policies, will find some of these principles already applied through such procedures as systematic personnel reviews. Others are up to him.

Jobs to Be Defined

Employees, from part-time porter to assistant manager, want to know what is expected of them. Written job descriptions meet a part of this need.* Unfortunately, they are not always available and complete. The descriptions that were accurate and complete when the branch was first opened may be a good deal less so even a single year later. Jobs change with the passage of time.

Any branch manager will be wise to make a point of reviewing the job descriptions for his staff, say, twice a year, to be sure they

* For examples of such definitions, see Appendix C.

are up to date. Since this chore is more vulnerable than most to the hazard of being crowded out, it is a good idea to put the item on one's calendar and then, when the date comes up, either assign the task or plunge in.

Good policy, whenever a new executive joins the branch staff or whenever a present employee is promoted, is to review the responsibilities with that individual personally. The newcomer's predecessor may have gone over the ground with him already, but if the manager also does this, two purposes are served. First, there is a double check on the new person's concept of his job and a chance to eliminate any possible confusion about where his responsibilities begin and end. More important, there is concrete evidence for the new appointee that the head of the house is interested in helping him get off to a good start. Young or old, a newcomer welcomes a show of friendly concern at this stage of his career. It can be the foundation of a loyal, enthusiastic attitude toward the store.

People Need Accountability

People need to know to whom they are accountable and by what standards they will be judged. The branch store's organization chart, with its criss-cross lines of responsibility, poses a bit of a problem in many areas. Orders come from several directions, and opportunities for conflicting instructions abound.

There is for example, the department manager. He usually gets orders from two or more buyers at the main store. He gets orders, too, from the next ranks above him at the branch. Occasional collisions of interest are bound to occur. One buyer may want a stock count urgently. Another may be sending in new merchandise for an upcoming promotion, with instructions to brief the salespeople and set up displays. The demands from the two buyers may come just at a time when a branch executive has laid down the law about improving service to customers. In the midst of all this, the department manager may be wondering what to do about an unanswered request for a fill-in on basic stocks. To follow up on the buyer concerned could be construed as criticizing one of his bosses. Superlative work rarely materializes under conditions of this kind.

One organization prevents such situations by telling its branch employees firmly that they have one boss, and one only—the branch manager. Cooperation with buyers is expected from them, and buyers are expected to give cooperation also. The difference between extending cooperation and taking orders is made clear. So is the fact that promotion, if any, depends on the recommendation of the branch manager.

In this organization, a branch manager's stature in the eyes of his staff is imposing. He is the one who settles disputes, and who follows up on requests all the way up to the vice president, if the cause is just. He is the one and only person to whom all branch executives are accountable. He occupies a position of leadership.

People Need Criteria

When work is routine and repetitive, it is fairly easy for the employee and his supervisor to judge his performance objectively. The only criteria necessary are the number of units handled, and the degree of accuracy achieved.

Not many of the jobs at the branch, however, can be measured by simple criteria. Yet employees, at whatever level they function, need to know what is considered good work. Without some guides, they swing toward perfectionism and anxieties, or toward indifference and slipshod ways. Things need to be spelled out for them.

Consider, for example, a salesperson who is told to keep the stock in order by straightening it out whenever customer traffic slows down. What is "in order"? It can mean one thing in a salon operation and another in a self-service area. What is "a lull in customer traffic"? Is it when there are no customers at all, or when there are fewer customers than salespeople, or when the customers appear to be lookers not worth stopping stock work for?

If branch management does not spell out such details to the salespeople, and do the same for parallel problems in other jobs, an employee may find himself reprimanded for doing something no one told him was wrong, or for neglecting something that no one told him was part of his job. And an unjust reprimand, no matter how tactfully administered, is a fearful squelcher of enthusiasm.

As one goes up the executive ladder, the nature of the details to be spelled out will change, but the importance of the spelling-out process does not diminish. For example, if a junior executive is rated on his ability to make a creative contribution, he should know that this is expected of him. Otherwise, he may hold back, for fear of treading on sensitive toes. Not only will he withhold a possibly useful contribution, but he will end up feeling unappreciated, and sure that no one realizes how capable he could be if given the chance. Both employee and branch are the losers in such cases.

People Need Checking

One of the cleverest training directors in retailing has a simple slogan: "Don't expect. Inspect!"

Inspection, formal or otherwise, is basic to good leadership. The manager who notices a spotless department and praises the salespeople for it has made them feel that their conscientiousness in keeping it shipshape is worth while. Conversely, the executive who sails indifferently past a messy area without turning a hair is simply asking for more of the same. People need to know that someone other than themselves is concerned with the way in which they do their work.

It is not necessary personally to praise or correct the individuals concerned in every instance. A word to the executive in charge of the activity, with instructions to pass along the comment, has much the safe effect, and also helps get the supervisor in the habit of speaking out to his people with commendation or criticism, as needed.

In a large organization, however, where rank-and-file employees tend to feel unnoticed, it is especially effective if praise travels the direct route. The occasional spot check, or neighborly look-see, or even military-style inspection by the head of the house has the advantage of letting people know that they and their work are important to the branch manager.

A former president of one of the world's largest stores applied this principle consistently during his incumbency. He made a point of inspecting each department in person occasionally. Usually, his planned visits were leaked carefully and well in advance. Each inspection became an opportunity to praise, as well as a lesson for the salespeople on the importance of their work and their department to top management.

People Make Mistakes

We all make mistakes, especially when we are young and new in our jobs. A good manager recognizes that one of the risks in his own job is to allow the people under him to make their quota of unavoidable errors—but also to make sure that they learn thereby. Honest errors are part of the learning process. Careless ones can be checked. Those that come about as a result of sheer indifference are not to be tolerated.

When the error comes to light and the employee must be corrected the branch manager is called upon to demonstrate leadership in the highest degree. It is not enough merely to apply the familiar rules about never letting subordinates hear a superior criticized and never to find fault in public. Something more is needed.

Psychologists say that a certain amount of hostility lurks even in the friendliest of manager-subordinate relationships. They suggest that, to work in the face of this latent hostility, corrections should be a judicious blend of fact and motivation to improve.

If, for example, a department manager has a poor record of keeping basic stocks filled, the recommended approach would be to cite the figures on the number and frequency of outs—not to begin with, "You're doing a pretty sloppy job . . ." or "You always seem to be out of sizes . . ."

Facts leave no room for argument. If they are reviewed with the employee, it is an easy transition from stating the case to seeking a way to prevent its recurrence. The experts also recommend finding a way to link correction of a fault with prospects of promotion. The procedure then becomes: statement of fact, motivation for improvement, search for methods of improvement.

The merely fault-finding approach tends to leave the employee embarrassed, hostile, unwilling to offer explanations, and often too upset to profit by suggestions for improved work. The factual approach invites the employee to participate in the discussion and may bring to light circumstances that contributed to the error and that may have escaped notice up to this point.

People Need to Grow

Part of the leadership responsibility of a branch manager is to recognize and encourage those people who are capable of growth and to prepare them to move ahead. Retailing sorely needs executive talent, and the branch manager who does his share in locating and developing such talent earns the appreciation and recognition of his own top management.

Students of management suggest procedures on this phase of the branch manager's leadership responsibilities. The young executive, they say, should learn to assess situations and make decisions of the kind he will be called upon to do in the job ahead. In short, he should practice for that job before he is actually assigned to it.

The advantage of this procedure is that, when the day does come for the step up, the young executive is more sure of himself and less likely to panic or to fail to recognize the key elements in a situation. Another advantage is that, if the manager has observed the person handling problems similar to those to be met in the new job, he can make or withhold recommendations for advancement with a feeling of security. The candidate for promotion is less of an unknown quantity to his superior than he would otherwise be.

Exercises in decision-making and situation-analyzing need not be of the classroom variety. They may be as casual and informal as, "How would you handle this?" or "Which would you buy?"

tossed in the young executive's direction during the day's work.

The discussions that arise in the wake of such questions require a little extra time from the branch manager, naturally. If the junior suggests a course that is not acceptable, there is an obligation to explain why it is rejected, and why the preferred course is the more profitable one to follow.

Yet this is time well invested. There is the satisfaction of helping a young person on the way up. There is the opportunity to earn approval from top management by contributing talent to the organization's promotional pool. In the interval before a suitable promotion opens up, the manager enjoys the help of a more valuable assistant than he would have had without this development effort. Finally, when he does make a recommendation for promotion, he knows that his candidate will be equipped to perform in a way that reflects credit on the branch and on him.

Setting a Model

Successful executives have been known to hark back to their "papa in the business"—some supervisor or employer who took a special interest in them when they were beginners and who set their feet on the right path. The "papa" may have done no more than suggest books to read, or courses to take, or ways to tackle a job. But by his interest and his example he made himself a model for the future executive and stirred up enthusiasm to make good.

However little a branch manager may care for the role of hero or "papa," it is more or less thrust upon him by the fact that young people on the way up do examine their superiors with an interested and analytical eye. Other executives at the branch have to bear the scrutiny only of their own staffs; the branch manager has everyone's spotlight trained upon him.

If he does no more than remain conscious of this conspicuous position, he will be meeting a good part of his leadership responsibility in this area. The junior executives in his unit should see him as loyal to management, concerned for the welfare of subordinates, and thoroughly enthusiastic about his own job. To seem callous, or bored, or critical of management is to forfeit the respect of these valuable youngsters and to diminish their eagerness for growth.

Some Don't Grow

Every tribe needs Indians as well as chiefs. In the branch store, there are bound to be plenty of Indians—people who either are not capable of further growth, or for other reasons wish to take on no additional responsibilities.

To such people, recognition and friendly personal contact mean a great deal. Further substantial money incentives and higher rank are not likely to come their way. A sense of their personal worth and importance needs to be developed nevertheless.

In dealing with these employees, any branch manager can learn much from politicians. The politicos are never too busy or too preoccupied to acknowledge the man in the street as an individual, or to speak to him as a friend or neighbor.

Time for hand-shaking is, necessarily, limited; yet whenever the branch manager shows himself on the selling floor, he has an opportunity to greet those who catch his eye—by name, if he has the fortunate gift of memory in that area, or with a friendly remark. "Nice day," or "How've you been?" are small things indeed, but they can help dispel the notion, treasured by many people in obscure jobs, that nobody knows or appreciates them.

If this sounds small-town and corny, it is. But so are many of the people who work in these dead-end jobs, and they thrive on such treatment.

Recognizing Ability

There are other ways to encourage people in minor jobs.

One is to recognize any special abilities by assigning some appropriate special work occasionally. For example, one branch manager has a few former secretaries on his sales floor. These are women who prefer part-time work and limited responsibility while they raise their families. But now and then, they love being asked to help in the office. They enjoy knowing that their skills are remembered and needed, even though these skills are not used in their daily work.

Contests, of course, can do wonders. Personnel departments usually have plenty ideas for activities in which everyone in the store can participate, and in which prizes are within anyone's reach. If there isn't much of this going on at the branch, a suggestion to the branch personnel executive, or to the personnel office at the main store, should stimulate thinking along these lines.

If they do nothing else, contests alleviate the boredom of routine jobs. At their best, they focus attention creatively on suggestion selling, error prevention, courtesy, charge account solicitation, and similar subjects.

Awards for individual excellence also help. A day off, a gift certificate, or even a special boutonniere, presented with a flourish, can be given for perfect attendance, error-free work, or good performance on any other front. Every employee should be offered some chance to win distinction in his own work.

Eliminating Irritants

Small irritants are great destroyers of morale, particularly among people in small jobs. No one can afford to make a career of tracking down every draft, or balky register, or other cause of unhappiness to an individual employee, but a good executive should certainly police areas of potential annoyance that are likely to affect large numbers of employees. Washrooms, rest areas, employee parking facilities, cloak rooms, cafeterias, for example, should be inspected regularly by the manager or a trusted lieutenant. And it doesn't hurt to let people know that such inspections are made in their behalf.

Some managements make a practice of seeking out causes of discontent and eradicating them before they become serious. Breakfast chats with rank-and-file employees from all over the store are a popular means of bringing small irritants to the surface for correction. Such chats have also, as a by-product, occasionally produced helpful suggestions for dealing with store problems.

The head of one large business house follows a procedure that lends itself to branch store use. Every week or two, he takes his lunch in the employees' cafeteria, carrying his tray with the others. The effect is to keep the food service on its toes, enhance employee pride in the facility, and underscore the approachability and interest of the top executive.

Good leaders brush no one aside as unworthy of cultivation. Little people as well as executives, little projects as well as major undertakings, all require the branch manager's attention if he is to build a unit whose employees are enthusiastic, alert, and productive.

CHAPTER 3

MAINTAINING EFFECTIVE COMMUNICATIONS

Branch managers, as a rule, are deeply conscious of the importance of maintaining good communications—of exchanging ideas and information with others, both in and out of their own units. A branch manager has to become a fairly adept technician in the field of communication, in order to:

- weld the people of his unit into a smoothly functioning organization,
- contribute to a climate of growth in his branch,
- maintain effective liaison with the parent store,
- convey the store's image clearly to its customers and its many other outside contacts.

Other chapters of this book discuss communication in terms of public relations, promotion, merchandising, credit, personnel relations. This section concerns itself primarily with what the branch manager does to improve communication inside that "people business," the retail store.

The Many-Directioned Flow

Experts on the subject often speak of communications as a two-way street—the flow of ideas, objectives, policies, and information *down* from top management through the various levels of responsibility, to the lowest ranks, plus the flow of observations, suggestions, and possible grievances *up* toward management from the lower echelons.

In branch management, to speak in terms of merely a two-way flow is to understate the problem. The branch, of course, shares the problem of maintaining clear channels of up and down communication with other business organizations. But, in a branch, at every level of authority, there is also a need for communication back and forth between the outlying unit and the parent store. The criss-cross lines of communication are rather like the appearance of a plug switchboard when every trunk and every extension is in use.

Everyone Has a Language

Good communication requires an understanding of the other party's language. In the Tower of Babel that is created by the varied objectives and capabilities of the individuals who comprise a store staff, there are many languages to be mastered, many overtones to be listened for. For example, consider the difference in impact upon a buyer of saying, "We're all out of...." and "Those numbers just walked out of the store." The first implies criticism, because, to a buyer, being out of a wanted item represents poor management. The second is a compliment to the buyer's ability to select. The first inspires resentment; the second, enthusiasm. Both sentences express the branch's meaning, but each carries a different connotation to the buyer.

Obviously, then, to achieve good communication it is important not just to express oneself, but to put oneself in the other party's shoes as far as possible, and address him in terms of his own interests, objectives, and responsibilities. When one does this, there is little likelihood of falling into such errors as trying to motivate middle-aged part-timers in terms of glowing opportunities for advancement, or seeking to attract young career trainees with promises of retirement benefits.

In his many-sided communication efforts, the branch manager has many languages to learn: to speak to buyers in terms of planned figures and volume opportunities; to speak to management in terms of long-range growth objectives; to speak to sales-people in terms of semi-annual salary reviews and small extras; to speak to young executives in terms of how the branch is a show-case for their talents. And more!

Communication, it should be remembered, is not always of the mass variety. The branch manager, it is true, has many occasions for addressing groups of employees personally or via the written word, but he also has innumerable occasions to get his message across to individuals.

In both cases, the important point to remember is that com-munication is not self-expression; it is a matter of transmitting a message on the other party's wave-length, even if that wave-length does not happen to be the most convenient and familiar one to use.

Spelling Out What Is Meant

Vital to good communication is knowing what one wishes to say, and then spelling it out. It is surprising how often people sidestep these prime essentials. The same individuals who would not dream of ordering a meal by saying, "Bring me lunch," will give instructions to business associates in terms even more vague than that. They tell executives to "get on the ball"; salespeople to "make an all-out effort"; vendors to "see what you can do to help"; and housekeeping aides to "get this place clean."

At the root of the vagueness and resulting failure to communi-cate is failure to think out first what is wanted. Here are some examples from actual store experience in hiring and directing salespeople:

STORE A. People were to be hired to staff a self-service operation —largely stock work and cashiering. Instead of asking the employ-ment office to hire customer service clerks, the store management used the familiar "salesperson" description of what it wanted. Applicants were interviewed, hired, and trained for selling, only to find themselves set to work at such (to them) unsatisfying tasks as manning cash registers and straightening stock. Poor communi-cation resulted in poor staffing and poor morale.

STORE B. A high fashion store urged its salespeople to give

apparel customers every possible personal service, down to bringing a cup of tea into the fitting room. It paid its people on a salary basis. Neither in its stress on service nor in its compensation plan did it communicate that it wanted, very much so, to see an increase in sales. The increase did not materialize.

STORE C. A fashion store wanted aggressive selling and decided that multiple sales were the best means of stepping up volume. It hired salespeople on commission only, and offered a higher rate of commission on multiple sales than on sales of single garments. Management's message got through loud and clear; the floor was staffed with pros; management got the high average sales and the high total sales figures that it wanted.

Spelling Out Job Responsibilities

A particular problem in branch communications is the matter of job responsibilities. Written or verbal, job descriptions can be clear and friction-preventing, or they can be poorly expressed, and thus constitute invitations to trouble.

In so many branch assignments, an employee works *under* one executive and *with* another. If the distinction isn't made clear, a relationship that was meant to be collaboration may become one of supervisor and assistant. Prime example, of course, is the department manager, who is usually expected to work *with* the main store buyers, but sometimes finds himself working *under* them— taking orders, running errands, doing chores.

Part of the branch manager's communication problem in such cases is, first, to make sure that each person at his unit understands the complex relationships correctly, and then to make sure that identical messages have been conveyed to the main store executives concerned. If correction is needed at the main store, his communication problem becomes one of deciding what needs to be done and then casting his request in terms of the aims and objectives of the person at the main store who can do the correcting.

Communication in the matter of job descriptions doesn't stop, of course, with spelling out responsibilities and clearing up ambiguities. It extends also to matters of approval, criticism, and correction, whether they are given verbally, in writing, or in the form of salary adjustments. The earned increase speaks volumes; so does the one justly withheld. Reprimanding an employee for poor performance and then increasing his pay is poor communication; so is praise, the loading on of extra duties, and the failure to recognize the increased load in terms of pay, rank, or privilege.

Getting What One Wants

An example of how to achieve results with good communication was provided by a branch training director who needed merchandise information for the salespeople at her unit. She wrote to vendors for help and amassed, almost overnight, a library of useful material. A large part of the success of this effort must be credited to the letter that communicated the store's needs. It stated the aims: to establish a reference library of available merchandise information for training meetings. Then it spelled out what it wanted: any information that would make a good sales presentation, such as what the merchandise is, of what it is made, for what it is used, how it can best serve a customer's needs, and what special features it has that will make the customer enjoy using it —plus any fashion or other story behind the merchandise.

Good communication is explicit.

A branch manager could encounter situations that make demands for good communication in, for example, a shopping center that has fallen into slipshod habits. Instead of asking the center manager or merchants association to "do something to make our center more attractive," he might spell out what should be done: maintain uniform levels of window lighting; maintain uniform hours for keeping windows lighted; landscape or repair landscaping in specific areas; ban certain types of window displays and encourage others; and so on.

Similarly, he may have the same problem of communication when he hires a contractor to clear snow from a parking lot. Is it to be cleared completely, or will it do to leave some portions un-cleared? Will it be all right to leave piles of snow in designated spots, or is all snow to be carted away?

And similarly, he may have a problem of communication when the time comes for employee reviews and ratings. The ratings given by supervisors will be meaningless unless they understand what they should expect of the people under them and how they are to appraise performance. Part of good branch communication is to call supervisors together (personally, or through the branch's personnel officer) before each rating period and make sure that each one understands the purpose and technique of the review. To make sure, it may be necessary to ask questions that will measure the degree of comprehension—and to recognize that those who give parrot-like responses are probably memorizing rather than understanding what was said. If any supervisor fails to get the message, the branch manager's communication channel with rank-and-file employees is less than clear.

Communications and Employee Relations

Good communication is an essential foundation on which to build good employee relations. It is not, of course, absolute in-surance that employees will be happy and well motivated, but it definitely improves the chances of avoiding conflict between man-agement's and labor's aims. If people know what they have been hired to do, how they will be judged and compensated, and what management offers, there is a sound basis on which to build.

Some of the poor communications rocks on which employee relations programs have foundered include these:

• Management lacks clear communication *from* employees and offers benefit programs that are not welcomed.

• Management lacks clear communication *to* employees and fails to make clear the virtues of benefit programs that are pro-vided.

• Management confuses employee contentment with earnings and benefits with what it really wants—motivation and the desire to do a better job. A person can be contented and secure, but lackadaisical nevertheless.

• Management fails to communicate to its hiring executives the skills required for the job. The result is employees overqualified and unhappy, or underqualified and inefficient on the job.

• Devices and gadgets, like conference telephones, taped messages, and filmed presentations are confused with actual communication. The physical means cannot alone insure that the message will be received. Also needed are a clear definition of what is to be conveyed and the ability to convey it in terms that will be understood.

• Communications are in terms of management's values—volume, profits, growth, store image, place in the community, etc.— rather than in terms of the employee's values. These may be security, money, job satisfaction, growth, etc., according to the individuals concerned.

• Efforts to improve communications are sporadic, or are attempted on an inadequate budget, or are based merely on what other stores have done. Good communications are achieved with continuing effort on the part of everyone, from top management to porter.

Barriers to Communication

An important element in communication is to recognize that certain barriers exist, and these cannot always be swept away. If one knows the barrier is there, and if he cannot find a way around it, he can at least make allowances for it—as one allows for the noises of static in radio.

One of the stubbornest of barriers is what the head of one major store calls the "status barrier." This is the constraint that naturally exists between a rank-and-file employee or even a highly placed executive and the head of the firm. No matter how eager a top management man is to unbend, the people below him never forget that he is at the top. And he himself must recognize the divisive influence of one simple fact of business life: if a policy decision is to be made, ultimately he is the one to make it, not the people below him.

The branch manager himself is in a position to experience the status barrier from both sides of the fence: in his dealings with his own staff, and in his dealings with his parent store's top management. He may not be able to remove that barrier in his own branch, but he can make allowance for it by recognizing that it may cause his people to be less than spontaneous in their discussions with him, and that it may also cause them to accept his casual suggestions as edicts.

Because of the status barrier, it is often a good idea to set up committees and discussion groups made up as much as possible of people of similar rank. They can then thresh out a matter freely and their chairman, in the capacity of spokesman rather than individual, can carry the consensus to management.

Close-to-home example: In some organizations, all branch managers meet regularly, either at the parent store or in one or another of the branches, to discuss common problems. Or they may meet regularly with the vice-president in charge of branches, who is their link with top management. In some cases, one branch may suggest a solution to another's problem. In other cases, the problem may exist in all branches and require attention from management at the main store.

Close-to-home possibility: Monthly meetings of department managers, with a senior department manager or the assistant branch manager as chairman, for free discussion of job problems.

Some Tools and Techniques

Although large-scale programs for improving communications may have to originate with the store's top management, there are many procedures that he can institute at his branch without waiting for a major effort. Among them:

Dealing with New Employees. Send a welcome note or greet personally on the first day. Outline the employee's job, including whom and under what circumstances to ask for additional advice and instructions.

Staff Meetings. Instruct supervisors, if necessary, in how and for what purposes to conduct meetings. Ask for reports. Provide out-

RESPONSIBILITY BULLETIN

Event   Fashion Show on Suburbia Mall

Dates   August 15 at 2:00 P.M. / August 16 at 3:00 P.M.

Person Responsible	Item	This bulletin to:
Miss A	Bulletin	Mr. Manager
		Miss Fashionist
Miss A	Contests, Gimmicks	Miss Buyer
		Mr. Div. Manager
Mr. C.	Employee participation	Misses Dep't Manager, Salesperson
Miss D	Interior Display	Salesperson
		Mr. Promotion Manager
Miss A	Meeting	Mr. Branch Display
		Miss Personnel
Mr. C	Models/Rehearsals	
Mr. E	News Releases	
Mr. F	Newspaper Advertising	
Mr. C	Public Address System	
Miss D	Signs, Windows	

Communication: Every step in preparing for and executing a promotion is listed, with the name of the person assigned. Each person on the list at the left receives a copy of the bulletin; each person on the right also receives a copy. Every one knows what he is to do and who is assigned to the other tasks involved in the project. Responsibility is fixed.

EXHIBIT 6

lines, suggestions, materials. Listen in occasionally and comment on achievements.

Getting a Feedback. Invite employees to use suggestion box. Report back to any who sign their contributions. Hold workshop sessions for small groups of employees engaged in similar work, so that they can discuss ideas and report back through the session chairman. Insist upon exit interviews with all employees who leave, and review the reports of these interviews occasionally. Ask merchandise department heads to furnish regular reports, possibly once a month, on best items, nature of cooperation received from buyers, etc.

Getting Merchandise Information. Ask buyers to send memos, no matter how brief or informal, on all new merchandise planned for branch. Ask for market bulletins, where appropriate. Encourage cooperation from buyers by:

• reporting back promptly on trends and other points of interest to them,

• offering criticism in the friendliest possible way, with every effort to avoid the appearance of sniping,

• acknowledging graciously all assistance provided,

• making them feel completely welcome on their visits to the branch.

Using the Written Word. In all signs and bulletins, use the simplest, clearest language possible. Accompany instructions with check-lists, forms, and any other devices that make compliance easier. Post all standing instructions, such as "Notify Mr. X of any packages that are damaged," near work places of people to whom they apply.

Using the Main Store Staff. Invite executives of main store to address branch personnel to reinforce branch training in fashion, salesmanship, credit, merchandise presentation, inventory taking, basic stock procedures, etc. Ask some to speak to rank-and-file; others, to groups with specialized jobs. Offer the branch as a testing ground for new merchandise, ideas, procedures, promotion techniques—one way to communicate a desire to cooperate cheerfully!

Making Assignments. For promotions, inventory-taking, and other projects, make explicit assignments—distributing and posting what one executive calls "responsibility bulletins," listing each person's job. Provide worksheets, forms, and any other tools required to do the job well. Set a deadline. Require a report.

Post Mortems. Past experience is a valuable guide to future planning. Ask all who participated in major seasonal events, who worked through Easter and Christmas peaks, who helped take inventory, etc., to report on:

- what was done right and should be repeated,
- what was done badly and should be done better,
- what was a mistake and should not be repeated,
- what was customer reaction.

Rank-and-file employees, as well as executives, may be able to contribute helpful ideas. Provide simple, friendly forms on which to note comments. Insist upon prompt reporting, before the details grow dim.

Keeping in Touch. Have a house organ, even if only a mimeographed page, for the branch. Maintain a lively bulletin board, with timely notices, touches of humor, suggestions for doing a better job, cartoons.

Scooping the Snoops. Undue secrecy on the part of an executive tends to develop prying habits in his subordinates. Not every part of the branch manager's job is public property, but whatever can be told should be told, frankly, to those who are entitled to know. Common causes of uneasiness and subsequent snooping include: rumors of cutbacks in employment; rumors of expansion plans; unusual hirings and firings; indications of slack business; indications of more business than the present plant and staff can handle. "We are working on the problem" is often a sufficient reassurance to check worry, disaffection, and prying.

J. L. BRANDEIS'
DEPARTMENTAL
CHRISTMAS DIARY
NOVEMBER 15 TO DECEMBER 31, 19—

The value of this questionnaire is self evident. Please complete it while the Christmas selling season is still fresh in your mind. It is imperative that the completed form be returned to this office no later than *January 23, 19—*.

* * * * * *

1. ADVERTISING—Good Fair Bad (Circle one) If "fair" or "bad," explain how they could have been improved. Be specific.

_____

_____

_____

2. Were events properly timed? (Give instances, if not) _____

_____

3. Were your ads in proper position in the newspaper? (Specify) _____

4. Cuts were— Fair Good Poor (Circle one)
5. Were these original or old Art? (Circle one) Original Old
6. Were ads proper size? (Specify, if not:) _____

7. Would you prefer fewer large ads, or more small ones? Large Small (Circle one)
8. Did you see proofs in ample time for correction? _____

* * * * * * *

1. DISPLAYS—Did you get enough window space? _____
2. Were your windows properly trimmed? _____
3. What suggestions would you make for improvements? _____

_____

4. Department Displays. What suggestions would you make for improvement of these? _____

_____

_____

_____

_____

* * * * * *

1. SALESPEOPLE—Did you have enough salespeople? _____
2. Were your salespeople properly trained? (If not, specify) _____
3. Do you have in *your* files the names of Christmas extras for next year's follow-up? _____
4. Will you take on a few Xmas extras earlier next year to insure a more effective selling force at the Xmas "peak"? _____

EXHIBIT 7 *(page 1)*

5. What suggestions would you make for improvement in this area? _____
_____
_____

* * * * * * *

1. STOCK PEOPLE—Comments and suggestions _____
_____
_____
_____

* * * * * * *

1. RECEIVING ROOM SERVICE— Good Fair Bad (Circle one) ·
2. Did the "do not mark" technique help you? _____
3. Did any selling confusion result? _____
4. Was your other merchandise marked quickly and properly? (Specify)_____
_____

5. Did you have lost shipments? _____
6. Are you satisfied with _____ as a shipment forwarder? _____
7. Could you get merchandise to the floor quickly? _____

8. What suggestions would you make for improvement of Receiving Room
service? _____
_____
_____
_____

* * * * * * *

1. SIGNS—Comments and Suggestions: _____
_____
_____

* * * * * * *

1. MERCHANDISE—What three classifications produced the most volume?
   1. Bought _____ Sold _____ Est. Purch. Next Year _____
   2. Bought _____ Sold _____ Est. Purch. Next Year _____
   3. Bought _____ Sold _____ Est. Purch. Next Year _____
2. List your three best *single items* in each classification:
   1. _____
   2. _____
   3. _____
3. Which ones do you think will be good next year (or an adaptation thereof)?
_____
_____
4. Which items were flops? _____
5. What classifications increased in sales production over last year? _____
6. What classifications decreased in sales production over last year? _____
_____

EXHIBIT 7 (*page 2*)

7. What "fringe" or "sleeper" items could be exploited next year in volume?
_____

8. What type of merchandise sold best in what spots? (Specify) _____
_____
_____   _____

9. Please attach to this report your Xmas floor plan of departmental re-arrangements.

10. What changes would you make in next year's re-arrangement? _____
_____
_____

11. Attach list of "outposts" you had this Xmas with exact record of dollar volume, also items used.

12. Attach list of "bargain square" items you had: by days, by items, by $ volume _____
_____
_____

13. Did you do any cooperative advertising? List: _____
_____
_____
_____

14. Did it pay off? (Specify): _____
_____

15. What approach should we take next year as to price lines, prices, brand-selling during the Xmas promotion season? _____
_____

16. Did you sell more or less branded goods? _____

17. Did your unit sale increase or decrease? _____ List devices you used to raise unit sale _____
_____

18. What was your experience with imports? _____
_____

19. How would you advertise them next year? _____

20. Christmas Catalogue items:
    1. Best items: 1_____
              2_____
              3_____
              4_____
              5_____
    2. Worst items: 1_____
               2_____
               3_____
               4_____
               5_____
    3. Why were the "worst items" worst? _____
_____

EXHIBIT 7 (page 3)

21. General comments for improvements of the catalogue: _____
_____
_____
_____

* * * * * * *

SERVICES—Please give your comments or suggestions on the following:
1. Elevators: _____
_____

2. Delivery—Packing: _____
_____

3. Breakage of Packages delivered: _____
_____

4. Christmas Boxes: _____
_____

5. Gift Wrap and Wrappers: _____
_____

6. Porter and Maintenance Service: _____
_____

7. Bargain Square Space allocation: _____
_____

8. Further General or Specific Comment or Suggestions: _____
_____

Communications: This Christmas Diary is an example of the post-mortem--a method of getting a feed-back from employees while the experience is still fresh in their minds. Similar forms can be worked up for inventory taking, other promotions, inauguration of new procedures, etc. The post-mortem is an excellent means of capturing constructive ideas and of converting grumbling into useful criticism.

(Reprinted with permission from The Buyer's Manual; Merchandising Division, NRMA-Revised 1965; pp 225-228)

CHAPTER 4

PUBLIC RELATIONS AT THE BRANCH

It has been said often and in many ways that no business does quite so much for its community, or depends quite so much upon the good will of its community, as does the retail store. Good public relations are as essential to the success of your branch as good merchandise, good promotion, and good service.

At a branch store, most of the burden of establishing and maintaining good public relations rests necessarily upon the manager. The downtown staff may have ideas, experience, and techniques at its command, but it usually does not have the essential intimate knowledge of local attitudes. In the final analysis, many of the key decisions will have to be his.

Personal Participation

As his store's ambassador on the local scene, the manager will probably join and participate actively in service clubs, merchants' associations, charities, and any other organizations that give him a chance to become acquainted with his community and make himself a part of it.

This phase of his work can be not only personally satisfying, but also extremely educational. Every time he attends a merchants' association or Chamber of Commerce meeting, he has a chance to exchange ideas with business men who, like himself, are studying and serving the community. Every time he serves on a charity board, attends a PTA meeting, or takes part in a community project, he learns something about his customers, and how they think, talk, dress and live.

If there are organizations in which he can take more than an ordinary share of responsibility, he should not hide his light under a bushel. He should let it be known that he is willing and able to pitch in, that he is amenable to heading a committee, or addressing a group.

For example, the nearby high schools may welcome a speaker on careers in retailing. Women's clubs, and even men's organizations, may be eager for a talk on wardrobe planning, home decoration, or other subjects on which a retailer can speak with authority. If they haven't thought of asking him, the manager should either make the offer on his own or urge the merchants' association or Chamber of Commerce to set up a speaker's bureau. In the latter case, the association secretary can suggest his name to schools, clubs, and other organizations.

Making a Talk

Not everyone is a born public speaker, but the art can be learned. If the field is new to him, the manager can begin his speaking career before small groups and limit his early ventures to those subjects for which he has the strongest enthusiasm. Skill and ease develop with experience. And they are worth developing. Each time he gives a talk that is favorably received, he is advertising his branch to and through his audience and making these people feel closer to the store than they did before.

In constructing a talk, it helps to think of it in terms of a group of three- or five-minute talks, rather than as one half-hour talk. This sounds easier, and it also serves another purpose: It keeps a speaker from going too deeply into any one phase of the subject. If forced to keep the treatment of each topic brief, one automatically avoids getting too technical or too detailed for a lay audience.

Whenever possible, it is good to brighten up a talk with exhibits, preferably of merchandise from the store. This is especially important in talking about fashion, either in dress or in home furnishings. Many of the incoming silhouettes, colors, and textures that are thoroughly familiar to retailers are still new to the audience.

Since technical descriptive terms may be meaningless to some of them, they will be glad to see what the speaker is talking about instead of having to rely entirely on verbal descriptions.

Usually, a discussion period is expected at the end of a prepared talk. Discussion, however, isn't always forthcoming on its own. A good safety device is to plant a question or two in the audience, or to ask the chairman of the meeting for the names of a few people upon whom to call for comment. The larger the audience, the more pump-priming will be needed before the questions begin coming spontaneously.

Working with Charities

Among the charities in a typical community, there are some that desperately need merchandising advice. In this group are those on the order of Good Will Industries, which solicits used, out-of-season, and damaged merchandise, and has the goods put into salable condition in workshops that teach its clients skills that will eventually make them self-supporting.

If no other merchant has stepped forward, the branch manager can volunteer to organize contributions among the retailers of his town or shopping center. He can offer himself as an advisor on the resale aspects of the enterprise, perhaps accepting a place on the charity's board, so that he can render constructive service.

There are also other community enterprises in which he can be of particular help because of his retailing background. As a business executive and large employer, he is especially qualified to work with organizations that seek to salvage school drop-outs or help deprived youngsters to move up a bit in the world.

Other charitable and civil enterprises may appeal to him for personal reasons, in no way connected with his business background. The opportunities to serve are many, even in the smallest communities.

Because he is the head of his branch, a manager's personal participation in these activities has a special plus: He sets an example for others on the store staff. Knowing that their boss devotes some of his time to such enterprises, employees at the store may come to him with suggestions for helping their own favorite charities. Some of the requests may be sound; others may be nuisances. But the very fact that he receives them is an indication that he is achieving one of his PR objectives—conveying the idea that the store is actively interested in the welfare of its community.

Relations with News Media

A part of public relations is publicity—getting the news about the store reported. There is more to this than simply mailing out press releases.

A branch manager can pave the way for news stories by building a good relationship with newspaper, radio, and TV people in your community. One way to do this is to make himself cheerfully available to them when they need opinions on business and fashion subjects. They call on people both for background material and for direct quotes. Before expressing an opinion, one should know for which purpose he has been asked.

Reporters and editors don't waste a business man's time. They themselves are busy people, and they know that others are busy, too. A friendly understanding with them can be built on a small investment of time.

Friendship alone, of course, won't buy you space in the papers or time on radio and TV. The store has to have something newsworthy to report. But by getting acquainted with the editors and commentators, one learns what news angles interest each, what their deadlines are, and so on. Then, when the branch stages anything from a kiddie party to a home furnishings clinic, the manager will be able to alert the appropriate local newshawks early enough to insure coverage. They, in turn, knowing him well enough to respect his opinions, will understand that he would not call them unless he had something usable.

Not to be overlooked among the news media: the store's own employees.

Particularly in suburban branches, where these people are drawn from many social levels, employees can spread the word effectively throughout a community. If the store has been made a pleasant, interesting place in which to work, their favorable attitude will reflect itself in their contacts with friends. By the same token, if they are properly briefed about coming events at the store, they can do their share in publicizing the branch's activities. And, being human, they enjoy the feeling of being insiders, in the know. Unless there's some reason for keeping a story under wraps until the last moment, it's good to make that feeling possible for them.

Political Activities

If a branch head has his management's blessing for going into political affairs beyond the simple requirements of good citizenship, there are many fields in which a retailer is especially well qualified to have an opinion and to take an active part in setting community policy. For example: education, traffic control, parking facilities, highways, local taxation, zoning laws. In larger communities, questions of urban renewal may come up, or of mass transit. All are of concern to a branch, and its manager will naturally want his voice to be heard when decisions are in the making.

Branch managers who have been active in local politics point out that consistent participation pays dividends. They report that, as a by-product of contributing time all along, they get interested attention when they offer an opinion. Other business men, who express themselves only when in danger of being hurt by some proposed regulation, are likely to find themselves unheeded.

Also important: To make the acquaintance of local police officials, to facilitate exchange of information and other cooperation between them and the store's protection staff in matters of mutual interest.

Store Activities

The amount of time and energy a branch manager personally can throw into public relations activities is necessarily limited, but there is almost no limit to what the branch, as a business, can do to improve its relations with the community.

Retailers are old hands at the art of staging public relations events. The procedure is exactly the same as for merchandise events, except that the objective is to sell, not goods, but the image of the store as a member of its community. Like a promotion, a good public relations event or continuing activity needs careful planning, explicit assignment of duties, thoughtful timing, and an honest evaluation of the performance and the results achieved.

The roster of possible events is enormous. The balance of this chapter consists of suggestions for branches drawn from the successful experience of other stores, including award winners in the annual "Retailing Serves America" contests run by Readers' Digest.

The suggestions are grouped by topic. Some may be suitable for use just as described. Others may touch off newer and better ideas for a branch. Old or new, activities of this kind can help put a branch store firmly and favorably in the community's eye. It pays to try them!

Youth Activities

Children's art: contests and exhibits.

Model building: contests and exhibits.

Dressmaking: contests and exhibits.

Summer dancing for teen-agers in store parking lot.

Easter egg roll.

Parties for handicapped children, at the store, or in institutions, with entertainment supplied by the store. Home talent, drawn from among store employees, is often especially good for this purpose.

Charm courses.

Teen advisory boards.

Exhibits and contests tied in with school work—historical, geographical, scientific, agricultural. School authorities are usually happy to work with the store in developing suitable projects.

Sports clinics.

Junior Achievement sponsorship.

Hobby shows.

Holiday parades.

Window decorating competitions in which contestants win awards for their schools or clubs, or do the windows for the sheer fun of it.

Fund-raising drives in which teen-agers and younger children can participate: by soliciting pledges, by manning booths, by performing services for pay, but with the pay going to the designated charity.

Hospital decorating efforts. Art students participate in decorating hospital wards at holidays, with materials and/or direction supplied by the store.

Contest among teens for the best youth activity suggested to the store.

Halloween at home. In a successful effort to reduce Halloween mischief in its town, one store invited young children to parade in costume, and teens to come to a costume party in the daytime. Prizes were awarded for the best costumes—but the youngsters had to stay home at night to wait for word by telephone as to the winners.

Lunches, dinners, etc., for special achievers in Boy or Girl Scouts, Camp Fire Girls, or 4-H.

Shows, musicales, ballets, staged at the store with the cooperation of school coaches.

Education

Cooperation with distributive education authorities in area.

Scholarship awards.

Sewing schools.

Cooking schools for boys as well as girls.

Science fairs.

Do-it-yourself instruction for girls as well as boys.

Salutes to local schools and libraries.

Students' day, when boys and girls take over key jobs at the store for a day.

Encouraging high school drop-outs among the employees to return to school. This can include the offer of counseling by store executives, adjusting hours of work, or even organizing after-hours volunteer coaching by members of the store staff.

Similar encouragement for high school graduates who indicate any interest in preparing for college entrance. Even putting catalogues of nearby colleges in the employee lounge can help!

Adult Education

Classes for adults—daytime, evenings, or Saturday mornings; in or outside of the store; for employees, or customers, or both; free or for a fee. Instructors may be recruited from branch or main store staffs, or they may be outside experts from magazine staffs, resources, schools, museums, invited by the branch.

Possible subjects include:

Business subjects.

Investments.

Use and appreciation of libraries, museums, or other local facilities.

Art and music appreciation.

Instruction in painting, sculpture, music, dancing.

Photography.

Gourmet cooking.

Health and nutrition talks; weight watching clubs.

Red Cross courses in first aid, child care, etc.

Gardening.

Flower arrangements.

Physical education; Judo.

Bridge lessons.

Golf, tennis, other sports instruction.

Interior decoration.

Needlework, dressmaking instruction.

Fashion and beauty courses.

Any other hobbies or sports currently popular in the community.

The Arts

Holding shows at the store for work of local artists—amateurs as well as professionals.

Photo exhibits of the same sort.

Loan exhibits of works of art from museums in larger communities, with or without guest lecturers.

Demonstrations of art techniques—paints, pastels, mosaics, ceramics, etc.

Folk music festivals, with possible help from music department of nearby school or college.

Charities

Personal participation of manager or other executive in fund drives.

Organized solicitation of contributions from employees.

Permission for solicitation of funds from public at entrances.

Devotion of one or more windows to subject of drive.

Contests for benefit of the fund. Example: Windows or Christmas trees are decorated, each by a different school, group, or individual. Customers vote for the one they like best—the vote taking the form of donation. Award to winner and amount of money raised for the fund are announced simultaneously.

Making store headquarters for merchandise donations, as when used articles are requested.

Cake sales, raffles, held at the store for a charity.

Benefit fashion shows, held in or out of the store.

Providing talent to entertain in hospitals or at fund-raising events in or out of the store—home talent or professional.

Inviting representative "clients" of a specific charity to lunch at the store or in nearby restaurant during fund drive in their behalf.

Inviting orphans to preview Christmas toy department and to spend small amount of cash given to each one by the store.

Employee activities: dressing dolls for orphans; contributing holiday baskets to needy families.

Community

Organizing children's tours of local points of historical interest, with cooperation of schools.

Participating in voter registration and get-out-the-vote drives. One store made a window available as a registration booth.

Participating in or initiating of safe-driving campaigns.

Days in honor of each of the various communities in area.

Awards to outstanding mothers, fathers, Scout leaders, etc.

In fast-growing community, the use of windows and ad space occasionally to acquaint newcomers with town's facilities and points of interest.

Saluting important local anniversaries; recognizing important dates and events in area history.

Participating in blood bank drives. Making window or spot near entrance available for registration. Use of infirmary, if possible, for donations. Drive among employees for donations. If local blood bank regulations permit, maintenance of a store blood "fund," to which some employees contribute, but on which the families of all may draw in emergency.

Annual Women's Day—luncheon, forum, or both, for club women of area.

Customer advisory board. Gertz, Jamaica, has had one for more than 25 years. The formula: Presidents of major clubs are members of board during their term of office. They submit customer complaints and suggestions to store management at monthly luncheons. Meetings also include buyers' clinics, at each of which one buyer explains how to buy a specific category of merchandise intelligently.

CHAPTER 5

THE SHOPPING CENTER

The retail environment presented by a suburban shopping center is unique in that each store's business is every store's business. The manager of a branch located in a shopping center, therefore, cannot be content merely to supervise what goes on within his own unit's four walls. If his branch is to achieve maximum volume and profit, he finds himself obliged to look beyond its doors and into the affairs of the center and its tenants.

The center's principal and often only magnet for attracting customers is the combined drawing power of its tenant stores. True, the center offers easy travel and parking, but so do others. The attraction that draws a customer to one rather than to another location for one-stop shopping is a balanced mix of merchandise and services, compatible with her wants.

Tenants at a center are usually chosen so that they complement one another and so that each helps his neighbors generate customer traffic. If any tenant, large or small, is laggard or slovenly, all suffer. Similarly, if the center is well kept and attractive, the customer enjoys shopping there and is likely to return. If it is neglected, uncomfortable, or dull; if parking is a problem; or if its stores offer assortments not geared to her taste, she has no reason to come back. There are other centers.

Leading the Center

A department store or specialty store branch is usually the dominant store in its center, and is looked to for leadership by the center management and the other tenants. As the largest, or one of the largest, stores in the group, it has more to gain or lose than any of them through the success or failure of the center as a whole.

In accepting the role of leadership that is thrust upon the manager by his store's position in the center, he may find himself walking a tightrope. He cannot afford to seem pushing, lest he will evoke resentment in his smaller neighbors. And he can't afford to slip into the background, or he will seem indifferent.

Some branch managers have found this happy solution:

Just about every center today has a merchants' association, supported largely by dues levied upon each tenant in proportion to the space he occupies. As the largest retail dues-payer, the manager of the department store branch is usually offered the presidency. Some make a policy of refusing the honor, but of serving as permanent vice-presidents.

In this way, the smaller merchants are forced to take turns at the top job. Knowing that they will have an experienced, bigstore retailer on the sidelines to help, they are less reluctant to take on the responsibility than they would otherwise be. Many of these men develop a surprising talent for leadership during their terms of office. In time, the branch manager and the center manager find that these ex-presidents constitute a body of stalwarts, able to help the center cope with any situation that comes up.

The Merchants' Association

Merchants' associations at shopping centers are generally formed for the primary purpose of joint action in the cause of attracting the customer. So valuable have these organizations proved themselves that current leasing practice requires all tenants to become members and specifies in the lease what dues shall be paid. Dues are generally in proportion to store area, with a sliding scale downward for very large stores. The center management itself may also contribute, possibly to the tune of 25 per cent of the annual budget.

The associations serve many functions, the most fundamental of which is that of promoting the center. A not unusual arrangement is to hire a promotion director, answering to the tenants, but cooperating with the landlord's center manager. Through this director, events to attract customers to the center are planned—merchandising events, public relations happenings, or anything else that will keep people aware of the center and bring them back to it repeatedly.

Association dues of, say, 15 cents per square foot per year, usually make possible a promotion budget adequate for such events as hobby shows, fashion shows, flower shows. Also for salutes to special groups, like 4-H and Boy Scouts. Also for engineering joint action among the tenants in selling periods like Easter, Mother's Day, back-to-school, and Christmas. Without the association, without its annual dues and its manager or promotion director, there would be need to solicit funds and cooperation afresh on each occasion for center-wide action. And the branch manager, representing one of the largest stores at the center, would probably have this impossible task added to his many other responsibilities. The chances are that very little could be done without an association.

Using the Machinery

Once established and functioning, the merchants' association at a center provides machinery for handling many of the problems that beset the stores there. For example, there is the matter of contributions and other requests from local charities and organizations. It is not the easiest thing for an individual store to refuse donations, or to sidestep requests to set up a booth for soliciting funds from customers. Yet there has to be a limit.

Some centers use their merchants' association for this purpose. They agree upon a figure for a center-wide donation—sometimes upon a series of figures, adjusted to the size of the organization making the request. The merchants' association manager then handles all requests, taking the onus from the individual stores. When door-prizes and similar merchandise contributions are solicited, some centers donate gift-bonds, redeemable at any store within the center. The practice appears quite acceptable to the organizations, the prize winners, and the merchants.

Requests for booths are also handled at many centers through the merchants' association. Some set aside a small area for this purpose throughout the year, and assign it to a different organization each week. Others, particularly those with large enclosed malls, turn a huge area over to all the organizations it can hold for a single week each year and thus create a traffic-generating bazaar.

The management of the community meeting hall is another task that can be taken over by the merchants' association. The center management may build and equip the hall, but the merchants' association takes over its maintenance and arranges the bookings. The rewards are good will, publicity, and unending traffic.

One center, with a hall whose top capacity is 150, reports use by more than 12,000 people in a single month, with activities going on from early morning until late at night. Users include classes of many kinds, both for children and for adults; parties; church groups; and even the local AA. News of meetings and events at that same hall generated over 6,000 column inches of publicity in a local weekly paper, over a year's time.

The Association as Spokesman

Not the least of the association's virtues is its capacity to act as spokesman for the entire body of tenants. There may, for instance, be occasions when the landlord is less than conscientious in the performance of his obligations, or when the tenants wish to suggest new services or attractions. Often, whatever needs saying can be said quietly and informally, by the merchants' association manager in his contacts with the center's manager. In most cases, requests or complaints come with better grace from the association than from individual tenants.

The association can also speak to its individual member stores in behalf of the center as a whole. Stores that do not observe the hours that the rest keep, or that do not hold up their end on advertising or participation in events, or that are lax in keeping up appearances, are among those that need to be spoken to. And here, too, requests or complaints come with better grace from the association than from individual merchants.

The association can serve also as a forum, at which all the merchants of a center can discuss center-wide programs of advertising and promotion and decide what each one's share of the financial and merchandising responsibilities will be. General questions of merchandising and promotional strategy can get an airing here, too, and large as well as small stores can benefit from occasional exchanges of opinion about economic conditions and trends in customer demand in the area.

The Shopping Center Manager

An important man in the branch manager's life is the shopping center manager, the executive who represents the owner of the property. One authority on shopping centers strongly advises the branch manager to make the acquaintance of this executive promptly, to study him, and to make a team with him in dealing with center problems and opportunities. With his background in retailing, the branch manager may be able to help him to understand tenant problems; he, in turn, can probably contribute a background on centers in general and this one in particular.

As a principal retail tenant, the branch manager is often in a position to recognize a problem and suggest a solution directly to the center manager before the situation becomes acute enough to inspire group action on the part of the tenants. Similarly, the center manager may have ideas for a promotion, or a service, or a new type of tenant to be sought for the center, and may welcome a chance to use the branch manager as his retail sounding board.

The better the center manager does his job, whether it is keeping the lawns green or eliminating an undesirable tenant, the easier it is for the branch manager to do his job of building his unit's future. Both executives have much to gain by making themselves available to one another for friendly, off-the-record advice.

Knowing the Ground Rules

In formal or informal collaboration with the shopping center management and its tenants, it is important to know the ground rules—the terms of the branch's lease. Unless he knows them, a manager may involve his store in expenses it does not have to meet; he may coax where he has the right to compel, or insist where he does not have the right to ask.

Even if he has previously functioned in one shopping center and is now assigned to another, the branch manager cannot take the provisions of the lease for granted. Whether the parent store owns the center or is a tenant like other stores, current leases may contain clauses quite different from those that were written a dozen years ago.

The lease under which a branch unit operates may prove to be a document so formidable that the manager must call upon the store's legal advisor to select the few points that most concern him, and to give them to him in straightforward language. Among those questions on which he needs definite answers are:

- What are the boundaries of the store property?
- How are responsibilities divided between store and center as to maintenance of grounds? Repairs to building? Snow removal? Exterior lighting? Protection?
- What sales, if any, are excluded from the total in calculating the basis for paying rent? This is particularly important to know if there is occasion to arrange for vending machine installations, leased departments, and profit services.
- What membership and dues are required of the branch and other stores at the center with respect to the merchants' association?
- What are lease renewal dates and terms? If the manager has suggestions for changes, he should know when a new lease is to be negotiated so that he can pass his ideas along to management in good time.
- How are store hours set and changed?
- What provision is made for employee parking?

• What participation in center events is required of the store? What minimum advertising outlay, if any, is required of the store and others in the center?

Unless he has all the details that concern the relations between his branch and the center, the branch manager may call in a roofer to mend a leak that the center should have repaired, or complain about the neglect of his store's parking lot when the store itself is responsible for maintaining that area.

The Manager as Go-Between

A branch manager functions as a go-between in several areas.

To the smaller stores at the center, he represents big store know-how, and they may seek his advice on merchandising, display, advertising, and other problems. If he is in a position to do so, and gives the advice, or gets the needed information from the experts at his main store, he is being more than just a good neighbor. He is doing his branch a service, too. Whatever helps the small stores at the center to increase their attractiveness to customers also helps the center and the branch.

He is the go-between, also, in the matter of keeping the main store's merchandising and promotion staffs aware of developments at the shopping center that concern them. He may hear, for example, that other stores there enjoy good demand for types or price lines that are only thinly represented in the branch stock. Or he may find, from neighboring stores, that the timing, or the response to certain types of displays or promotional appeals, is different among their customers from the pattern his store had anticipated. These are all points for him to carry back. He can help his main store to use the experience of other stores at the center as a supplement to whatever his own sales and stock records show.

The center's schedule of promotions and events is, of course, something to carry back promptly to the sales promotion executive at the main store. If he is experienced with shopping centers, he will probably ask eagerly for just this information and also the manager's personal recommendations for tying in. Promotion directors whose stores have branches at several different shopping centers ask each branch manager to develop a promotional calendar for his unit—one that is compatible with both the individual shopping center's plans and those of the downtown store. With this, and similar calendars from the other branches, the promotion staff can function with top effectiveness.

On the other hand, if a branch is the first shopping center venture for an organization, the initiative for coordinating center and main store plans may rest with the branch manager. As rapidly as he learns how the shopping center's promotion and demand patterns differ from those of the downtown store, he will have to relay the information to the downtown promotion staff. He will become a major source of information for them about shopping center programs, local media, and whatever else they need to know in order to serve the branch effectively.

Experts on shopping center management have at times criticized top retail management for failure to adapt merchandising and advertising approaches to the needs of their suburban branches. When such criticism is leveled at a branch, the fault may well be the manager's. With good liaison on his part, his management should know his branch, his customers, his center, his retail neighbors. Failure to adapt need not happen if the manager meets his obligations as go-between.

Promoting the Center

It is to the branch's best interests that the shopping center should have a balanced diet of promotional events and public relations activities. These should be scheduled well in advance, so that there is ample time for everyone at the center to prepare and play his part.

Public relations events like those listed in the chapter on that subject are excellent for the center—often even better than for a store alone. As center undertakings, many such projects can draw upon the talents of financial, medical, and entertainment people among the tenants, as well as upon retailers. Facilities for handling large crowds are generally better, too, than when an individual store underwrites the project. The mall, the meeting rooms, the parking lot, can accommodate many more than a branch store auditorium.

Suggested Events

Suggestions for events, both public relations and of the kind meant to produce immediate sales, follow:

Suggestion-box sale. Invite customers to drop suggestions in ballot box. Run sale of most wanted items.

Community catalogue, with merchandise from all stores in center. Direct mail, special section of local paper, or giveaway.

Free gift-wrap days. Special tables at which customers can gift-wrap purchases themselves with special shopping center gift paper.

Child health days, child beauty contests.

Days dedicated to 4-H or Scout activities, with exhibits or demonstrations planned by leaders, and with awards to outstanding members, nominated by the organizations.

Mother's Day luncheon for outstanding mothers and foster mothers, nominated by local women's groups.

Father's Day cook-out, with recognition of fathers nominated by local service clubs.

Father-and-son dinners or Saturday luncheons. Mother-and-daughter tea parties or luncheons.

Teacher's day, with luncheon or awards for outstanding teach- ers, selected by local principals or state education associations.

Woman-of-the-year contest, with non-retail judges. Award merchandise and services from center. Tie-in with newspaper or broadcast media is usually desirable.

Favorite program ballot. Invite shoppers to vote (blanks obtainable in stores) for favorite radio or TV programs. Personality representing favorite show to be invited to center after voting ends.

Meet-the-celebrity promotions. Endless variations, from popular writers to sports stars.

School athletic contest, with ballots obtainable in stores and prizes given by center to outstanding school athlete of year. Saturday morning award ceremony, with stores featuring teen and younger clothes, plus sports gear.

Foreign trade events, dedicated to a country, a continent, an area of the world, or the whole idea of foreign trade. Each store to highlight some import merchandise. Bank to show foreign coins and currency. Teachers to have children prepare appropriate exhibits, to be shown in store windows.

Anniversary sales for the center.

Mystery bargain days, when all stores feature unannounced specials.

Health check-up days, when local health agencies or doctors at center's own medical building check all comers free for diabetes, tuberculosis, high blood pressure, heart conditions, etc. to tie-in with special national and local health weeks.

Beauty contests for teens or younger children, with merchandise prizes. Have outsiders act as judges!

Reward-your-salesperson days. Give each shopper a card, or print coupon in newspaper ad. Shopper gives up card or coupon to most helpful salesperson. Salesperson with most cards wins merchandise bond award.

Thanksgiving turkey raffles, ticket with each purchase made in two weeks preceding drawing.

Treasure chests, keys with purchases during specified period.

Guess-the-number contests. Marbles, coins, beans, in glass jar; award to one whose guess is closest to number; purchases sometimes required to qualify for entry.

Free trip-for-two contests, with purchase usually required to qualify for drawing.

Garden club exhibits, with home merchandise events running concurrently in stores.

Made-it-myself fashion or hobby shows, with concurrent merchandise events in store.

Summer fun exhibits of boating, swimming, water skiing, fishing, and concurrent promotions of sporting goods, beach fashions, back yard pools, etc.

Dollar days, with each store offering a limited number of door-buster specials.

Brand name day, with each store offering limited number of discontinued numbers from known lines.

Full-tank promotions, when every receipt for a purchase above a specified amount is worth a free gallon of gas at the center's filling station.

Stagecoach days, with western actors on the scene, stagecoach and pony rides for the kids, and big merchandise promotions of children's wear.

Buy-in days, with posters and pickets on the mall, calling attention to bargains offered.

Outdoor cooking contests, to coincide with promotion of summer wear, sports equipment, patio goods, etc.

Fashion shows, fashion shows, fashion shows! For men, women, children. With professional or volunteer models. For charities or just plain business-building, with as many stores as possible providing garments and accessories.

Secretaries' day, salute to business women, nurses' day, salute to mothers-in-law—any reasonable excuse to salute a group of women and present fashion and home furnishings shows in line with their special interests.

CHAPTER 6

MERCHANDISING THE BRANCH

Retail management assigns to the merchandising staff the responsibility for inventories and assortments. Yet, as branches develop in size and number, and as each unit develops individual characteristics in response to the demands of its own clientele, it becomes increasingly necessary for the branch manager, too, to play an active, creative role in merchandising.

The Merchandising Job

The merchandising job consists of several phases. In simplest terms, these are:
1. To analyze customer demand;
2. To seek out the merchandise customers want;
3. To balance inventories against customer demand, store image, and financial considerations;
4. To present, promote, and sell goods;
5. To observe and react to competition.

In a single-unit store, the buyers, under the direction of their merchandise managers, can shoulder all five phases of the job readily. When branches enter the picture, however, and geography rears its complicating head, the buyers encounter the problem of performing these functions without being in close touch with the various selling floors. They need from each branch a flow of information that will help them plan for it and serve it intelligently—just as each branch needs information from buyers about future plans and present merchandise.

To facilitate this flow of information, it is important for the branch manager and department heads to understand the buyer's function, what he can do, and what he cannot. With this background, the manager and department heads are not likely to overlook vital developments that should be reported, or to overemphasize trivial ones. Neither are they likely to contribute to a climate of irritation by demanding of buyers that they do things that are impossible or beyond the scope of their authority.

Analyzing Customer Demand

The buyer's principal tools in analyzing customer demand are:

1. Records of what sold, at what prices, and at what rate, in previous seasons. Records of unfilled customer requests, if any.

2. Observations of what other stores, particularly those in direct competition, have sold successfully, and offer in their assortments.

3. Information on trends of demand. Sources include: other buyers in the store; buyers of other stores; buying offices; resources; trade and consumer publications; fashion advisory services; whatever else may be available.

4. Observations of the store's customers, how they live, and what changes in their way of life may be foreshadowed by conditions in the area.

The branch manager can help give the store's buyers an accurate picture of branch demand in these ways:

1. Insisting upon accurate and complete compliance with sales record systems. This may involve, depending on the merchandise:

(a) Collecting stubs of sales tickets,
(b) Copying detail from tickets to sales checks,
(c) Punching detail from tickets in to cash registers,
(d) Counting stock for periodic or special inventories,
(e) Entering counts, receipts, etc., on basic stock and other records.

2. Insisting upon care in checking receipts and transfers of merchandise. Errors in recording the amount of stock received can

give a distorted picture of branch sales and inventory, as well as contribute to shrinkage.

3. If the store has a system for recording unfilled customer wants, making sure salespeople and department heads understand its importance to the buyer and to the branch. If the store has none, take the initiative in developing one.

4. Watching for and reporting low and out of stock conditions. Sales will not reflect customer preference accurately and completely if they are made from assortments which are badly lacking in what customers want to buy.

5. Watching for and reporting customer comment and reaction to the merchandise offered.

6. If any items are outstandingly good or outstandingly poor sellers, not waiting for the buyers to dig this information out of the routine records that reach their desks. Passing the word along specially.

7. Watching for and reporting relevant activities of competitive stores, and also of non-competing merchants in related fields.

8. Keeping the merchandising staff posted on the changing interests of branch customers and any other factors that may influence their purchases.

Seeking the Merchandise

If the buyers have an accurate picture of customer demand at the branch, they usually know where and how to obtain the wanted merchandise.

There are occasions, however, when a buyer cannot give a branch what it asks for. For one thing, if he believes that an item has only limited and local appeal, he may decide against stocking it. The buyer for a multi-unit store seldom wants to nibble at what the market offers; either he buys a style in a range of sizes and colors, or he leaves it alone. Competition may have an exclusive. If the line is important, the buyer will provide his own close substitute.

A buyer for a multi-unit store, moreover, cannot always change his plans quickly and at short notice, to accommodate a local situation, in the way that a small independent can. He has his commitments made well in advance, with regard to the needs of several different units in as many different communities. These commitments are made with an eye to future as well as present needs; to a balance between what is required tomorrow as well as what is wanted today; to a balance between concentrating a share of the store's purchases with major resources and using some of its funds to develop fresh sources of supply.

A wise buyer will report back to the branch on his decisions and the reasons behind them, if only to keep the requests and the information constantly coming. Some stores insist upon a procedure of this kind. They consider all branch requisitions, whether for fill-ins or for items not previously stocked, just as if they were orders, and the buyers, vendors. Each requisition must be acknowledged and either filled or refused with reasons.

If the store has no such system, the branch manager can get much the same effect by asking his department managers to confirm all merchandise requests to the buyers in writing, and to note the dispositions on the carbons.

Spot-checks of the carbons from time to time will tell a great deal, and will show up situations where the manager may need to step in: the buyer who consistently ignores requests, for example, or the department manager who makes endless trivial or unjustified requests.

Such checks may also help bring to light an emerging pattern of change in customer demand at a branch—for higher or lower priced goods, for large or smaller sizes, for a neglected style in home furnishings. Many of the checks will show nothing significant, but in others, this bit of merchandising radar may begin showing significant blips worth watching.

In addition to following up on merchandising requests to buyers, the branch head should check at intervals with department managers to be sure that buyers keep them informed of incoming goods, of merchandise they consider especially salable and of numbers they plan to return to vendors. It is important to follow up on those buyers who are remiss in this respect.

Managing the Inventory

Inventory management in the retail store is a well developed science. When the merchandising staff has an adequate indication of customer demand, and when it has related that demand to both the store image and the availability of merchandise in the markets, it draws up plans that are designed to keep the size of the inventory at any given time in line with all these factors, plus projected promotions, plus that very important element, the financing of the merchandise investment.

Merchandise plans are usually drawn up twice a year, about 60 to 90 days before the start of the six-months period they cover. A plan is made for each department or classification separately. The departmental plans are assembled, like a mosaic, into a division-wide, and then storewide plan. The plans made for each branch must fit into those for store organization as a whole.

How a Buyer Plans

Buyers draw up their plans, first in units and then in dollars, working with their merchandise managers. Sales are estimated first for each tiny subdivision under the buyer's management, and then for whole departments or classifications.

In projecting sales, the buyer considers such outside factors as fashion trends, general business conditions, economic trends in the area, price trends, conditions in the markets involved, the competitive situation, promotional plans, and so on. Internal factors are also weighed: expansion or modernization plans, possible changes in departmental size or location, etc.

Sales goals are set, month by month, for the main store and each of the branches, and for the entire operation under the buyer's jurisdiction. If the branch manager is consulted in the setting of his branch's sales figures, he should prepare himself for the planning session with carefully organized information on local conditions. He should be ready with whatever data he has collected

Branch Store Plans

(BOJ-FOJ-MOJ-POJ) · **SEASON MERCHANDISING PLAN**

DEPT.

		LAST YEAR	PLAN	AGE OF MERCHANDISE	LAST YEAR $	%	PLAN $	%
Initial Markup	%			FASHION 1-3 MOS.				
Markdowns	%			FASHION 4-7 MOS.				
Shrinkage	%			FASHION OVER 7 MOS.				
Workroom Cost	%							
Gross Margin	%			NON-FASHION 1-7 MOS.				
Discount on Cost Purchases	%			NON-FASHION 8-13 MOS.				
Gross Margin Plus Discount	%							
Turnover				NON-FASHION OVER 13 MOS.				

			FEB. AUG.	MAR. SEPT.	APR. OCT.	MAY NOV.	JUNE DEC.	JULY JAN.	TOTAL SEASON	AUG. FEB.
SPRING. 19___ FALL. 19___										
SALES	BOJ	LAST YR.								
		PLAN								
		REVISION								
		ACTUAL								
	FOJ	LAST YR.								
		PLAN								
		REVISION								
		ACTUAL								
	MOJ	LAST YR.								
		PLAN								
		REVISION								
		ACTUAL								
	POJ	LAST YR.								
		PLAN								
		REVISION								
		ACTUAL								
RETAIL STOCKS 1st OF MONTH INCL INVOICES	BOJ	LAST YR.							*	
		PLAN							*	
		REVISION							*	
		ACTUAL							*	
	FOJ	LAST YR.							*	
		PLAN							*	
		REVISION							*	
		ACTUAL							*	
	MOJ	LAST YR.							*	
		PLAN							*	
		REVISION							*	
		ACTUAL							*	
	POJ	LAST YR.							*	
		PLAN							*	
		REVISION							*	
		ACTUAL							*	
TOTAL SALES		LAST YR.								
		PLAN								
		REVISION								
		ACTUAL								
TOTAL STOCK		LAST YEAR								
		YARDSTICK								
		PLAN								
		REVISION								
		ACTUAL								
3 MONTHS STOCK-SALES RATIO		YARDSTICK								
		PLAN								
PLANNED RECEIPTS		PLAN								
		REVISION								
		ACTUAL								
MERCHANDISE MARKDOWNS		LAST YR.								
		ACTUAL								

APPROVED___
A438° Rev. 2   MERCHANDISER   *END OF PERIOD STOCK PLUS INVOICES   BUYER

Reprinted with permission from the Buyer's Manual
NRMA, 1965; Revised; p 148

EXHIBIT 8

from news media, banks, schools, and other merchants, to substantiate his opinions. Points to bring up include: construction plans in the community, new competition, possible changes in the age distribution, income changes, expected lay-offs or expansion among major employers, and so on.

Once the sales estimates have been made, month by month, other pieces of the mosaic fall into place: the markdowns likely to be needed each month; the stock required to support the sales and provide the desired turnover; the amount of purchases to be received into stock each month. On these points, too, if the manager has relevant data to support his opinions, he will have a better chance of having his suggestions heeded. He may have that data in his personal notes and observations of stock conditions, customer reactions, and other factors at the branch—points that sometimes do not show up plainly in the cold figures on last year's sales and stocks.

In its final form, the plan will include actual figures for the previous year, planned figures for the coming period, and spaces in which to insert actual figures as the new period unfolds. Some forms provide space for entering any revisions of plan that may later become necessary. Also set down are the desired initial markon, cash discount, and other figures that management may require of the buyer.

Open-to-Buy

Once the merchandise plan has been made and the buyer begins operating under it, constant watchfulness is exercised to see that purchases are kept within bounds. Once a month or oftener, the buyer is given an open-to-buy report, showing how much may be spent for the period ahead. A more accurate name would be "open-to-receive," since the report is concerned actually with how much additional merchandise may be brought into stock within the time limits of the plan.

The open-to-buy may be calculated at the beginning of a month, or in the course of one. The procedure is to add:

1. Planned stock for the end of the month, and

2. Sales expected to be made during the month, or the remaining part of it.

From this total, subtract:

3. Actual stock at time of calculation, and

4. Merchandise on order or in transit for delivery during the period.

Sales, markdowns, returns to vendors, and transfers from the branch reduce Item #3 and increase the open-to-buy. Incoming merchandise, customer returns, and transfers to the branch increase Item #3 and reduce the open-to-buy. Orders placed increase Item #4 and reduce the open-to-buy. Cancelations of orders have the reverse effect.

If a department has overspent, or has not achieved its planned sales, the buyer may not have enough open-to-buy to take care of branch requests for replenishment of stock. Because branch stocks are often too small to allow much margin for error, some retail managements will clear the field for branch needs, regardless of open-to-buy limits. This is a management decision, however, and not one that the buyer alone has authority to make. Conflicts between the branch's needs and the buyer's lack of open-to-buy in most organizations have to be referred to a higher level of command.

Model Stocks

A widely used planning tool is the model stock, set up once a season or once a year, to guide the management of a segment of the stocks. The buyer, with the approval of the merchandise manager, develops each model in the light of past experience and present judgment.

For basic stocks, a familiar procedure is to spell out, literally, the minimum and maximum number of pieces wanted in stock at any time for each style, size, color, and price. The minimum is set in terms of how much is needed to supply customer demand during the period between ordering and receiving replenishments. The maximum is set in terms of how often and in what quantities replenishments can be bought economically. Stock counts are taken at regular intervals. If items are at or near their designated lows, reorders are placed either directly or through the buyer to bring the supply up to the established maximums.

A group model is sometimes possible and desirable, especially in branches, where the emphasis is on keeping stocks small. The idea is to combine stocks of several similar items or styles into one model, provided that the items within the group are readily substitutable for one another in the customer's eye. It can prove easier to meet the customer's needs with, say, a combined stock of 60 pieces of three substitutable items or styles or colors than with three separate stocks, each of 40 pieces. Children's socks, for instance, might lend themselves to such treatment.

Model Stocks for Fashions

As applied to fashion items, the model stock is usually concerned only with the minimum number intended to be in stock at all times during the selling season. At the height of the season, the stock may be far above what the model calls for, but it will not intentionally fall below the model until clearance efforts begin.

For example, suppose a buyer is building a model stock for misses' car coats. In the $30 retail price, he may want two garments of a size, in each of five sizes, or a total of 10 pieces as a minimum. Various colors and styles may be distributed among the different sizes, but no one of them may be in all five sizes. In the next lower price line, he may want two of each of the end sizes, and four of each of the three middle sizes, or a total of 16 pieces as a minimum, in various colors and styles.

A model stock is an effective planning tool only to the extent that it matches the demands of the branch's customers. If the branch manager is consulted in the setting up of model stocks, he should come prepared with facts as to where the departments were over-stocked or under-stocked the previous year, and how this year's demand is expected to compare with last. Model stocks are at best, intelligent estimates of demand. They should periodically be checked to see if expansion or restriction is needed.

Unit Controls

Unit control systems tell the buyer how many pieces of a style, color, size, and price are in stock and on order, and how many have been sold. These are vital guides to present needs, and treasuries of information to use in future planning.

Systems used for items with high unit price, like furniture, fine jewelry, furs, and many kinds of outer apparel, literally follow the history of each individual piece of merchandise. They record the order, the receipt of the goods, the sale of each piece, and any returns from customers or to vendors.

If the controls are manual, a record card is assigned to each style. On this card, entries show the amounts on order, on hand, and sold. Entries are made in numbers or in tally marks, or both, and sometimes in a variety of colors—black for sales, red for returns, etc. If the style comes in different sizes and colors, separate blocks on the card may be used for each size and color. Orders, invoices, and sales slips or ticket stubs provide the information from which entries are made.

With a manual system, the buyer may have the records kept in his own office. Examination of the cards will tell him how things are going and where action is needed. In some stores, the records are kept centrally. Either way, summaries are taken off at intervals for the buyer's information.

Under an electronic system, the machine's memory takes the place of the record cards and tally marks. The buyer has no style cards to consult, but receives instead printed reports and summaries from the machine.

Manual or electronic, unit controls are no more accurate than the information fed into them. If salespeople are careless about ticket stubs and sales slips, the buyer can have only an inaccurate picture of the branch's experience to guide his activities in its behalf.

To encourage the needed cooperation, the branch manager should remind department managers constantly of the importance of accurate reporting. They, in turn, should remind the salespeople frequently, so that what might otherwise deteriorate into

VENDOR NAME	*Egelson Garment*				VENDOR NUMBER	*135*

Cost 51 75 Ret 89 25

Style #8175	AUG	SEPT	OCT	NOV	DEC
RECEIVED ¹		////			
8/6 –20 ²	//				
8/25– // ³	///				
⁴	/				
⁵					

	8	10	12	14	16	18
Black	X /	X X X	X ///	///	X /	
Blue		//	//	//		
Red		/	/	X /		
Tan	X	X /	//	/	X	

Merchandise received is listed twice –
first, date and total quantity received,
like 8/6 – 20 (as shown above)
size and color chart as above

Merchandise sold is tallied twice –
first, in the week of the month in
which it is sold as in the upper chart,
(note two tally marks in the second
week of August)
second, in the size and color chart (note
one size 8 in tan)

Reorders are tallied in green in the size
and color chart and then tallied over
in black when received. This will show
the outstanding reorders at all times.

Customer returns are tallied in red in the
size and color chart.

Returns to vendor are crossed thru in red
instead of black.

Printed with permission from the Buyer's Manual,
NRMA, 1965; Revised; p 175.

EXHIBIT 9

a meaningless chore retains in their eyes its proper status as a necessary, much used source of stock replenishment and information. Buyers can be asked to cooperate in the branch's drive for accuracy by reporting errors to the manager, so that he can take steps to prevent their recurrence.

Periodic Stock Counts

For many kinds of merchandise, particularly basics and items with low unit prices, periodic stock counts are adequate. The counts are made at regular, scheduled intervals and are entered in books, usually loose-leaf. There they are compared with the minimum-maximum figures of the models set up for the category, and any needed replenishments are ordered. At the same time, sales during the interval between counts are calculated and entered. (The calculation: To stock on hand at the time of last count, add any receipts of new merchandise, and subtract the present count.) Since the intervals between counts are presumably uniform, any marked variation in the sales figure is a possible indication of a change in the rate of demand.

Want Slips

No matter how capable the buyer and how excellent the controls, there are always occasions when customers request merchandise the branch does not have. Some of these requests make sense; others seem not to. The important thing is to educate salespeople and department managers to pass no judgment, but to record the requests for the buyers.

The usual medium for such records is the want slip—any simple form on which the salesperson can note the date, department, and a description of what was requested. Some stores also ask salespeople to try to get the customer's name, address and telephone number, with the understanding that, if the item does come into stock, she will be notified. This is not a special order, but just the offer of an extra, friendly service. Some want slips provide space for the salesperson to note whether she was able to sell a substitute.

Lost ... a Sale!

Because we were out of:

_____

_____

_____

Remember:

- A sale lost is money lost in commission.
- We don't know you're out of something 'til you tell us.
- Don't wait . . . tell us now before you lose another sale.

Name	Dept.	Sales No.	Date

- If no sales were lost, please so indicate by checking here ... ☐

9481-42

7Ⓐ4113N   The Baltimore Business Forms Co., Atlanta, Ga.   BUY-38

WANT SLIP

EXHIBIT 10

New items in the the market may announce themselves via the want slip route; the need for more generous stocks of certain sizes, colors, and prices may be indicated. Also, a wild idea or two that can be ignored may show up. But if wants are not reported, or if they are reported only on a hit-or-miss basis, the buyer can't know that the branch's needs are not being met.

```
┌─────────────────────────────────────────────────────────┐
│                          STORE                           │
│  TICKLER CARD      Date_____  SLNo._____      │
│                                                          │
│  NAME_____│
│                                                          │
│ ·ADDRESS_____.PHONE_____       │
│                                                          │
│  Item requested_____│
│                                                          │
│  Size_____Color_____Price_____         │
│    Follow-up & Results-Date Sold_____         │
│                                                          │
│  _____         │
│                                                          │
│  Contacted Customer_____         │
└─────────────────────────────────────────────────────────┘
```

Follow-Up on Wants. --At branches of a major quality specialty store group, when a salesperson reports a wanted item that is not in stock, she is encouraged to make out a tickler card like this one, for later follow-up. If the customer gives her name, and if the merchandise later arrives in stock, the salesperson telephones to report its availability.

EXHIBIT 11

Wise buyers report back to department managers and sales-people on the disposition of wants, to encourage continued alert-ness. Often a batch of want slips is the only indication a buyer can present to back up a request for a larger budget or a wider range of price lines and classifications in behalf of a branch.

Slow Selling Reports

Most buyers are alert to fast-moving items that need prompt replenishment. What they may lose sight of, however, are the slow sellers that remain in stock for days or weeks, and on which action should be taken before their salability is lost.

Stores usually code the season and week or month of receipt on the price tickets of merchandise, so that a quick glance will show up any pieces that are over-age. Reports from unit controls, manual or electronic, also help to keep the buyer aware of slow moving stocks.

In a branch with relatively small stocks, however, even a few slow starters can represent a large portion of the inventory—and a real problem. One store's branches handle things this way: When fashion merchandise is received, clerks mark a code number indicating the date on the back of the price tag. Then, any time a department manager or the branch manager himself looks through the racks, he has only to flip over the tickets to see which items have overstayed their welcome. In a matter of moments, a list can be made up from the price tags and sent to the buyer with a request for action.

If store system makes no provision for indicating the date of receipt on the ticket, the branch manager can have this done on his own initiative, with a code mark on the back. Reserve and non-marked stock can be dated on boxes and containers. Also, if he wants more frequent age analyses of his stock, particularly for fashion goods, than the store provides, the manager can arrange to have this done.

A quick procedure is to provide salespeople with columnar sheets, each column of which is labeled for a specified age code or group of codes. With these sheets, the salespeople go through the stock and note down only quantities and prices in the appropriate columns. Basic staples can be omitted. In the manager's office, the totals and percentages for each age grouping can be quickly calculated, department by department, or classification by classification. Trouble spots will stand out.

For those classifications or departments that have unduly large percentages of over-age stock, actual lists should be made up of the older items, with details of style, size, price, age, and quantity. Such lists become action lists, for discussion with buyers, and for appropriate effort. It is as much to the buyers' interest as it is to the branch manager's to identify and act upon stock that has been too long in the branch.

Shopping the Competition

Shopping the competition, consciously or unconsciously, is something retailers seem to do all the time. Going through another merchant's store seems to awaken the critical faculties and makes the mind more alert to ideas that can be adapted—or avoided—in one's own store.

In shopping a competing store with buyers' needs in mind, however, one should check, for each department or classification, such points as these:

1. Price lines—highest, lowest, most heavily stocked.

2. Values, and any specific instances in which they seem to be outdoing one's own store.

3. Promotions, reported preferably with clips of ads and indications of results achieved.

4. Assortments—styles heavily or lightly stocked, sizes, colors, etc.

5. Brands carried, brands featured.

6. Items given featured position in the department.

7. Items featured in windows.

8. Colors, silhouettes, types, given prominence in the assortment.

9. Any items in their stock, apparently doing well, which the

branch doesn't have. Any doing well at the branch, that the competition doesn't have.

10. Identical items at different prices.

More points suggest themselves as one studies the problems of a specific department.

The reports need not be formal nor need they cover all bases. For example, a department head may note that several good styles in the stock are moving well in all colors but pink, and then check what other stores are doing on the color front, and report the complete story to the buyer. Every bit of information, collected in a spirit of honesty and passed along in a spirit of helpfulness, does its share toward giving the buyer a clear idea of what is happening in the branch.

Special Branch Considerations

In merchandising a branch, certain factors which make the approach differ from that taken from a downtown unit must be considered.

Generally, suburban customers buy closer to time of need and therefore, merchandise should not be brought in as far in advance of a season as for downtown, nor cleared from stock as early toward the end of a season. Inventories of seasonal "basics" should be kept full closer to the end of the period.

Branches need a continual influx of fresh merchandise since their customers come from a narrower geographic area and shop more frequently than would be so for in-town stores. The shopper who sees the same merchandise time after time will lose interest in visiting that store. For the very same reason, it is not possible to take the same advantage of a "best seller" in a suburban store as one can downtown. A customer would begin to resent it if she saw the garment she bought on too many of her neighbors.

Of course, the degree to which these factors are significant decreases as the size and regional nature of the branch store increases.

CHAPTER 7

MANAGING BASIC STOCKS AT THE BRANCH

Basic stocks are the lifeblood of almost any merchandising operation. Basics, by definition, are items that enjoy such consistent demand throughout the year or any part of it that they should be in stock at all times, in complete assortment. Basics are items the customer has a right to expect to find whenever she shops for them.

Because of the consistent demand, sales of basic merchandise are reasonably predictable, at retail and at manufacturing levels. Manufacturers can produce such items at a steady rate, carry stock, and be ready to supply retailers at short notice. Retailers can function on minimum inventories, with frequent fill-ins.

Under such circumstances, markdowns other than those for soilage and damage are rare; turnover is better than the department's average; values are good. Profits, as well as everyday volume, are dependable.

How Basics Are Identified

Every department or classification has its share of basics, but what is basic for one store is not always basic for another. Small sizes may be basic for one; large sizes for another. Plain white, as in bed sheets and bath towels, may be basic in one store, yet scarcely salable in another. "Basic" is a relative term.

Common practice among department stores is for each buyer, working with his merchandise manager, to draw up a list, once a year or once a season, of the items considered basic in his department. Changes may be made in the list in the course of the season, if circumstances warrant.

Since the list represents items the buyer acknowledges as enjoying consistent demand, the merchandise office in many stores retains a copy of each buyer's list and checks departmental stocks at intervals to make sure that all items are adequately covered. In any but perhaps a high fashion store specializing in ultra-new clothes, basics are bread and butter, sure profits, rent-payers. Management wants them to be in stock.

In some stores, open-to-buy is separately drawn up for basics, so that any overbought conditions elsewhere in a department do not affect these vital stocks. In other stores, reorders for basics are put through without regard to the open-to-buy. And in some cases, the whole responsibility is left to the buyers; it is up to them to see that basics are covered.

A basic is not always a single item. It may be any of a group of items, more or less equivalent to one another in the customer's eyes. One brand or color of women's underwear briefs, for instance, may be able to substitute for another. If that is the case, then briefs of various colors and brands, in identical price lines and sizes, are considered as a single item. If flare-leg panties, however, are not substitutable for briefs, the presence of a strong assortment of this additional underwear style does not excuse the buyer's failure to provide briefs in adequate supply.

Identifying Basics at a Branch

The basic stock list that a buyer draws up for a branch is not necessarily identical with the one he has drawn up for another branch or for the main store. Tastes are different; incomes are different; ethnic composition of the population may be different. These and other variations make for difference in the kinds, sizes, and prices of items that are basic at an individual branch.

Here is where the branch manager can help. The lists drawn up by his store's buyers represent merely each one's best judgment of the items that will enjoy consistent demand in the months ahead. Such lists are neither infallible nor unchangeable. If the branch manager sees that they omit certain items he considers basic, or include some for which he anticipates little demand, it is to his advantage to bring the necessary facts to the attention of buyers and merchandise manager.

Basic stocks, it should be kept in mind, are those that the buyer will endeavor to keep in good supply throughout their selling season. A true basic that is omitted from the list may be inadequately stocked, with resulting loss of sales and profit. An item that is not basic but is stocked as such will tie up some of the branch's inventory, taking up space and investment that could be put to more profitable use.

The branch manager's observations and suggestions about what constitutes a basic for his unit should extend to sizes, colors, and prices, as well as to styles. For example, if the men in his area are burly types, his branch may need a maximum of large sizes in shirts, underwear, socks, and shoes; if they are predominantly slender types in white collar occupations, his branch may need smaller sizes and narrower shoes. Similarly, a woman's plain white handkerchief at 25 cents may be basic at one branch, whereas at another the demand may center at the 50-cent level, and in a third, there may be virtually no demand for unadorned whites.

Another possibility is that special circumstances in the branch's area may suggest certain items as basic that are not even carried in the main store or any of its other branches. For example, the proximity of a few large hospitals and nursing homes may make nurses' oxfords, white stockings, and uniforms basic at a branch, even though the downtown store is primarily a fashion shop.

How Basic Stocks Are Maintained

Basic stocks are usually maintained through the device of the periodic stock count. This means that the buyer specifies how often the stock should be counted and also indicates a point below which the quantity on hand should not be permitted to fall. When a count shows that the inventory is at or below this reorder point, the buyer arranges for replenishment.

In setting the reorder points, a buyer considers such factors as:

1. The average rate of sale of the item. Usually this is in terms of number of units sold per week.

2. The number of weeks required between placement of order and arrival of replenishments on the selling floor. This includes time required to process the order, time required for delivery from the resource (even if the "resource" is the main store's stock room), and time required for the goods to get from the receiving dock to the selling floor.

3. The amount of stock to be added to minimum requirements to cover the time that will elapse between counts, plus a safety cushion for unexpected delays.

Having established the reorder points, the buyer goes on to work out economical quantities for reordering. At each count, an order is placed for the designated quantity of each item that has fallen down to or below its reorder point. Thus, the stocks are expected to be maintained at the calculated levels.

What the Branch Can Do

The minimum stock levels, the frequency of counts, and the re-order quantities are set in terms of the buyer's best judgment. Like the basic stock list itself, these figures are neither infallible nor unchangeable. It is up to the branch manager and his department managers to observe the operation and seek action on flaws—whether these flaws are in the buyers' estimates or in the branch's performance.

For example, the buyer may have planned his basic stock for Item A in terms of a count every three weeks, and for Item B in terms of a count every second week. If the branch counts both at three-week intervals, Item B may well be out of stock repeatedly. Also, if the branch is slow about processing replenishment merchandise through its receiving routine and out on the selling floor, the stock may run lower than the buyer had anticipated. If slow processing is chronic at the branch, the buyer may over-ship or over-stock to compensate for the delays. In the former case, the branch loses sales; in the latter, it ties up more money than it should in inventory and slows turnover.

BASIC STOCK CONTROL								Classification_____						Page No.____		
Period From_____ To_____																
Count Date																
Order No. →								Sales Recap							Sales Recap	
Item No.	OH	OO	OH	OO	OH	OO	OH	OO		OH	OO	OH	OO	OH	OO	OH	OO

Simplest Basic Stock Control Form--This ultra simple form for entering branch basic stock counts illustrates the principles of control by periodic count. The form is loose-leaf, facing a page of description on the left. Item numbers are entered in the extreme left column. Count dates are recorded at the top. Orders placed are entered by number under the count date to which they refer. In the OH (on hand) columns, floor stocks are entered above the diagonal line, and reserve stocks below. Amounts ordered are entered in the OO (on order) columns, and circled when received. At specified intervals, sales recaps are made (on hand at first count, plus receipts in period, minus on hand at last count) and entered. Stock level, frequency of reorder, and rate of sale are obvious at a glance.

Where sizes and colors are important, each page can be used for a number, and each line for a size or color. Form can also be used to recap activity for groups of items from their individual count sheets.

EXHIBIT 12

If the branch manager sees that the system is producing excessive stocks, or out-of-stock conditions, or is requiring too frequent counts, or is presenting other problems, he should report the condition to the buyer for correction.

BASIC STOCK LIST

Store No. _____   Dept. _____   Inventory Cycle _____

ITEM – DESCRIPTION		COLOR	CLASS	MAT.	STYLE	RETAIL		VENDORS NAME			
SIZES											**TOTAL**
BASIC	FLOOR STOCK RES. STOCK										
DATE	INVENTORY COUNT										
	NEED										
	0.0 DATE DUE										
	BUY DATE DUE										
DATE	INVENTORY COUNT										
	NEED										
	0.0 DATE DUE										
	BUY DATE DUE										
DATE	INVENTORY COUNT										
	NEED										
	0.0 DATE DUE										
	BUY DATE DUE										
DATE	INVENTORY COUNT										
	NEED										
	0.0 DATE DUE										
	BUY DATE DUE										

SPECIAL INSTRUCTIONS

Basic Stock Control. For items that come in several sizes (or
other variations), this form controls the stock and shows the
rate of activity. A basic or model quantity is entered at the head
of the column for each size. After each inventory count, simple
subtraction shows how many units are needed. Outstanding orders
are consulted, and the amounts are entered on the third line. If
the on-order figure for any size is not adequate to bring the inventory
up to basic quantity, an entry on the "buy" line shows the amount of
any additional ordering to be done. A glance at the "buy" figures
provides an indication of the rate of sale in relation to the basic
quantity provided in inventory.

EXHIBIT 13

Organizing the Counts

A first, essential step toward getting better coverage of basics in the branch is to organize the counts required by the various buyers, so that they are done with clockwork regularity and without excessive demands upon any one person or department.

Left to himself, the typical buyer will probably ask for Monday morning counts. In a large downtown department with an ample sales staff, this is not impossible, and it gives the buyer a whole business week in which to try to get replenishments on the floor in time for the next weekend.

At a branch, however, where a small staff has to provide information to many buyers, it is wiser to distribute the counts throughout the week, if possible. And to make sure they are done!

A good tool for this purpose is a master chart with the days of the month down the side and the names of department managers or salespeople across the top. On this chart, each count required should be entered—weekly, bi-weekly, monthly, or whatever the frequency—on the line for the day when it is to be done, and in the column for the person responsible for seeing that it is done. In that way, the load can be distributed evenly, and with due regard to special conditions like vacations, heavy selling days, etc.

Other possibilities: Tickler cards for each month or week; calendars that show a week or a month at a glance; cards for each count, with tabs positioned to indicate the date of the next count. The tools necessarily vary with the branch manager's facilities and preferences, but he should have a system that tells him quickly how many counts are required, in what departments, and which people are assigned to them.

It is quite possible that a branch may be required to make more counts than it has people available and hours available for the counting. If rescheduling and replanning do not provide an answer, the situation should be brought to the attention of management. Additional help for counting and checking, or even a special staff to do nothing but make the counts, may be possible. The outlay should be able to pay for itself in added sales and improved stock turn through better protection against outs and overstocks.

Studying the Reports

The reports of basic stock counts are well worth studying. The usual control form on which counts are entered is one that shows the amount in stock at the previous count, any reorders and replenishments between the last count and the present one, and the present stock. Sales for the period between counts are calculated. (To previous stock, add any additional stock received, and subtract present count.)

These figures can tell the branch manager and his department managers a great deal:

1. *Zero stocks.* If an item has been out of stock even for one day, sales may have been lost. A special watch should be made of the rate of sales of that item, if zero stocks occur often, to see if the minimum stock figure has to be moved upward. The rate of sale may have increased; the time required to replenish stock may have lengthened; the period between counts may be too long.

2. *Zero sales.* Is the item actually basic? Or is it one of those sizes, colors, prices, etc., that are basic downtown but not in this branch? Other possibilities: The stock may be poorly placed or presented on the selling floor. Replenishments may have been so late that the department had nothing from which to make sales of this item for most of the period. The count may have been wrongly taken.

3. *Frequent reorders.* The rate of sale may be heavier than was anticipated, or the inventory may be unrealistically small. The reorder quantity may have to be increased. Frequent small reorders, especially if they come to the branch by direct shipment from resources, run up high transportation costs.

4. *Unnecessarily heavy stocks.* If sales are consistently low in relation to size of stock, it may be that the stock can be cut back, or that the item is not as much a basic in the branch as it originally seemed to be. Or it may need better presentation, an occasional feature display, or some other stimulant to sales.

Discussion with buyers on any of these points may produce improvement. In every case, volume, profit, and turnover are being jeopardized, and it is in the buyers' interests to work with the branch manager toward correcting the situation.

Vendor Counts

Many stores and many departments avail themselves gratefully of vendor aid in counting basic stocks. In such cases, the resource's salesman or an assistant comes into the store at regular intervals, counts the stock of the company's products, estimates what is needed to replenish the supply, and writes up an order for the buyer to sign. Typical is the service given by greeting card publishers, or by wholesalers of miscellaneous stationery or hardware items.

There is a natural tendency, when a vendor takes such responsibility, to leave the entire matter in his hands. This can be a mistake, because there is an equally natural tendency for vendors to manage basics in the light of national or regional demand, rather than in terms of demand at a specific branch.

Problems are created if the vendor's representative calls at the store too infrequently, or only at irregular intervals. Omitting scheduled counts, or leaving too long an interval between counts, can result in out-of-stock conditions on fast sellers, or in unnecessarily heavy stocks to provide for the lengthy interval between counts.

The branch manager, therefore, should at least spot-check any vendor-counted basic stocks as to (1) frequency and regularity of counts, (2) breadth of assortment in relation to branch needs, and (3) reorder quantities in relation to branch needs and stock space. Any situations that appear in need of correction should be brought to the attention of the buyer.

Direct Reordering

In a great many branches, some or all of the reordering of basics is done directly. Instead of sending the counts or requisitions to the buyer for action, the branch writes up its own orders for forwarding directly to the resources.

In such cases, the branch manager should make sure that the reordering is not done mechanically or carelessly. No order should be mailed until someone has checked it for:

- correctness of reorder quantity
- price
- terms
- shipping instructions
- date
- cancellation date
- correctness of vendor name, address, style number, etc.
- department number
- any other information required by store.

Other checks against carelessness suggest themselves, if not for every order, then on a spot-check basis among those that leave the branch: whether the quantity counted actually warrants a reorder; whether an outstanding order was taken into consideration; whether the stock on hand is so low that the order should be phoned or wired in; and so on.

The branch manager who forms the habit of scrutinizing these orders may find himself discovering troublesome but correctable situations. For example, some vendors may be chronically slow in deliveries, or may be addicted to partial shipments, or may be inaccurate as to colors, sizes, and quantities specified. These faults should be brought to the attention of the buyers concerned, and so should any favorable variations, such as when a vendor regularly take appreciably less time than was anticipated to replenish the branch stock.

To keep basic stocks adequately maintained on minimum investment requires constant alertness, not just on the part of buyers and department managers, but also on the part of the branch manager himself. Few aspects of merchandising are more important to the welfare of a store or its branches than the careful management of basic stocks.

CHAPTER 8

THE USE OF CLASSIFICATION DATA

The application of classification data is one of the many aspects of retailing about which a branch manager cannot afford to be other than well informed. He does not make the decision to compile the data; he does not set up the classifications about which information will be compiled; but he does have the responsibility for using the figures so that he wrings from them every possible bit of sales and profit help for his branch.

A Background on Classifications

The classification today is regarded as an increasingly necessary tool for indicating the direction that consumer demand takes among the immense assortments of merchandise now available. The department is too large a unit; its figures contain so many kinds and varieties of merchandise that they may mask important trends. Unit control records focus attention too closely on individual items; the forest may be obscured by the trees.

A classification is neither an item nor a department. It is a group of items, readily substitutable for one another as to end use from the customer's point of view. Emphasis is on the words "substitutable" and "customer." Merchandise is classified, not in terms of the market where it originates, or the material from which it is made, or the resource whose factories produced it, but in terms of the end use to which the customer puts it.

One can draw an especially obvious example from the major appliance field. Refrigerators, whatever their make, would be in

one classification. Ranges would be in another. A buyer or merchandise manager who looks at major appliances in general, or
who thinks in terms of brands, might not see the ups and downs
in sales of refrigerators or ranges as readily as one who watches
classifications.

Moving over to the fashion departments for an example, consider handkerchiefs and head kerchiefs. They could conceivably
be carried in the same department, and be bought by the same
buyer. Yet each is in a different classification, because the two
kinds of merchandise are not substitutable for one another as to
end use from the customer's viewpoint. A surge of interest in head
kerchiefs could be hidden in departmental totals, but not in classification data.

Some classifications, like men's topcoats, are usually contained
within a single department; others, like women's sweaters, may
cross department lines and turn up in several places within the
store. In either case, the classification reports are watched for
signs of shifting demand, gaps or duplications in the assortment,
and unexploited opportunities.

Classification Reports

Stores differ as to how much classification data they make
available to the branch manager and how frequently they send
reports to his desk. A store may provide nothing more than a
monthly report of how much is sold in each classification, or it may
give the manager an elaborate report of sales, stocks, markdowns,
and other details, with year-to-date totals, comparisons with plan,
comparisons with past year, and even more.

Even from the simplest of reports, however, the information,
when studied in the light of the manager's personal knowledge of
the branch and its customers, can guide him toward increased
volume and reduced expenses.

Studying a classification report is not easy, particularly for
someone who is new at it and is confronted with one of the more
elaborate products of electronic data processing. The amount of

Classification Report

MERCHANDISING BY CLASSIFICATION

FOWLER, DICK AND WALKER, WILKES-BARRE, PA.

MERCHANDISE POSITION
CLASSIFICATION REPORT

DEPT. NO. **651** DEPT. NAME **CHINA GLASSWARE** DATE **JANUARY 2 1965** WEEK NO **49** PAGE **1**

CLASS	COMMENTS	ALL PER	BASIC STOCK	WEEK THIS YEAR	PLAN	OVER/UNDER	WEEK LAST YEAR	Y.T.D	Y.T.D LAST YEAR	Y.T.D	Y.T.D LAST YEAR	STOCK ON HAND	ON ORDER FOR THIS PERIOD	REQUIRED STOCK	OPEN TO BUY
02	OPEN STOCK C S 2.00	52		343	13	330	13	3409	3859	832	195	3952	5	4026	69-
03	2.01 TO 5.00	52		10-	37	47-	37	1085	2169	3	109	2718	21	2149	590
04	OPEN STOCK 5.00 UP	52		33	19	14	19	6592	5908	132	134	11742	330	6441	5631
07	OPEN EARTHEN TO 1.00	52		43	4	39	4	1011	1138	126	9	408	.	1305	897-
08	EARTHEN 1.01 TO 2.00	52		92	43	49	43	6031	2085	357	1192	1045		2224	1179-
09	EARTHENWARE 2.01 UP	52		3	12	9-	12	3236	3318	216	167	3536	100	3609	27
11	CHINA SET UP TO 2.00	26		125	173	48-	173	7233	6325	1299	1467	2621		2529	97
12	CHINA 2.01 TO 5.00	26		395	175	220	175	8221	6967	735	758	5145	1680	4443	2382
13	CHINA SETS 5.01 UP	26		5		5		60	82			60-			60-
14	EARTHENWARE TO 1.00	26		208	73	135	73	10004	9100	919	1496	3926	298	5536	1312-
15	EARTH SET 1.01 2.00	26						355	90	165		236			236
16	EARTHWARE SET 2.01	26							16			143			143
21	CORNING PYREX WARE	16		107	73	33	73	10997	8486	107	126	3773	29-	2165	1579
22	OTHER DOMESTIC WARE	20		16	67	51-	67	2660	3633	80	245	2292		1440	852
23	IMPORTED COOK SERVE	20		1	17*	16-	17	646	617	9	78	62-		254	318-
31	DOMESTIC	16		6	26	20-	26	1460	2084	32	77	335		353	18-
32	IMPORTED	20		42	76	34-	76	3522	3322	590	607	1422	220	774	868
41	GLASSES TO .50	16		329	237	92	237	9022	5477	186	112	2941	1	1438	1504
42	GLASSES .51 TO 1.00	16		34	58	24-	58	1568	2176	291	693	944		441	503
43	GLASSES 1.00 TO 2.00	16		7	53	46-	53	799	1904	59	211	622	56	766	88-
44	GLASSES 2.00 UP	20		7	17	10-	17	1698	1305	90	140	2658	871	488	3041
45	GLASSES BOXED 5.00	16		115	25	90	25	3134	2862	205	160	3906	105	539	3472
46	GLASS BOXED 5.00 UP	16		42	66	24-	66	1217	1776	152	216	716		403	313
47	JUICE BEV SETS ETC	20		59	8	52	8	3391	3167	135	131	1972	40	956	1056
51	MILK COLOR DOMESTIC	24		137	117	20	117	10598	8141	415	217	2529	1756	2250	2035
52	OTHER DOMESTIC GLASS	18		134	49	85	49	6300	5724	165	125	3583	509	1273	2819
53	IMPORTED GLASSWARE	24		40	15	26	15	4295	3596	256	391	962	410	1564	192-
61	PLASTIC TABLEWARE	16		32	14	19	14	939	3563	115	587	208	1	1036	827-
86	CLEAN POLISH AGENTS	06						169	92			9		4	5
91	PROMOTIONAL TO 1.00	16		6	31	25-	31	1830	1776	49	112	118-		195	313-
92	OTHER PORMOTIONAL	16		10	40	30-	40	106	474	36	36	15		239	224-
95	REPAIRS AND SERVICE														-
99	POSTAGE			2	3	1-	3	2407	625	109		247-			247-
				2363	1541	824	1541	113995	101857	7865	9791	63872	6374	48837	21409

Reprinted with permission from the Buyer's Manual
NRMA, 1965; Revised; p. 189.

EXHIBIT 14

information, even for a branch with relatively few departments, is enormous.

Rather than try to absorb it all, it is simpler to scan the pages for figures that are outstandingly good or poor. In other words, the first step is to seek out and study the exceptions, so that one can make advance preparations for an impending boom or take corrective steps against an impending bust.

A secretary or an assistant can mark the figures that need attention, and save the manager at least these preliminary steps. He should provide guideposts, however. A simple way is to ask for a mark in colored pencil next to each of the three or five best and worst figures on these points:

1. Sales figures as compared to last year
2. Sales figures above or below plan
3. Stock figures as compared to last year
4. Stock figures higher or lower than plan.

When Sales Are Good

When classifications show exceptionally good sales figures, the first step is to check on the genuineness of the indications of growth. There may have been special promotions in these classifications, or competitors may have been caught napping, yielding up business by default. Or demand may be growing.

If there is reason to believe that one or more classifications have a legitimate uptrend in demand, the next step is to check with the department manager and, if necessary, the buyer, to see what is being done to capitalize on the opportunity.

Buyers can usually be counted on to notice and merchandise to a growth opportunity. If not, the branch manager is there to remind them. Either way, however, he has the responsibility for setting his own unit in order, and in as many ways as possible, to cash in to the full on the favorable situation.

If more stock and broader assortments are planned, he may have to reassign space and facilities, to give the growing classification room to expand. If this means cutting back on some less active department or classification, it is to be expected that there will be at least a token struggle from those that are yielding space. The branch manager's authority, his prestige, and his reputation for fair play make it easier for him to handle the reassignment personally rather than let an assistant step into an area of possible conflict.

The manager's good offices will make the path of progress smoother, also, if the classification merits extra window space, or displays in other departments, or the loan of merchandise from other departments for use as a background for displays in its home departments.

Preparing Salespeople

The branch manager's authority will be needed also in reviewing assignments of salespeople to prepare for the expected growth. Will more people be needed, or will it be sufficient to give a quick briefing to those at nearby stations, so that they can step in if a rush develops? Will outpost selling of the classification in other departments be desirable? In any of those situations, it may be advisable for the branch manager himself to say, "This is how I want it."

Merchandise training is doubly important in a growing classification. A request to the buyer can spark extra efforts in this direction—a branch visit by buyer or assistant, or by a resource qualified to teach, or the loan of booklets, films, exhibits, or other aids. If there seems to be a special opportunity, then a special request for help should be made.

In some instances, a growth classification may require changes in register location, wrapping and packing facilities, aisle space, fixturing, access to the selling area, so that customers can buy quickly and easily. Even if he does not expect crowds of Gold Rush proportions, the branch manager should make sure that no removable obstacle stands between the desirable classification and the customer.

He should, of course, put in a request for promotion to help along the excitement in the growth classification. There may also be further opportunities to explore, right under his own roof: telephone calls and post cards from salespeople to their personal followings, for instance.

The Profit Incentive

The incentive for all this activity is not just that additional volume is in the offing, but also that it is likely to be especially profitable volume. When sales come almost of their own accord, there is little need to shave prices or cut margins. Promotions bring better results. Advertising costs are proportionally lower for these than for other goods. Markdowns are fewer. Selling cost percentages are lower.

Another incentive, of course, is that by having wanted merchandise the branch improves its reputation among its customers for completeness of stock. The customer doesn't rate a store's stock in terms of size—only in terms of how accurately it serves her wants.

Looking for Related Opportunities

Because the branch manager has a storewide viewpoint, he will on occasion realize that a boom in one classification may indicate a similar increase in demand for another in a different department or even a different division of the store.

For example, if children's swim suits are booming, there is every reason to bolster the branch's stocks of water toys, life preservers, sun glasses, sunburn creams, and toy rafts. Or, if fine china sales have been moving upward, a check on a possible local trend toward more elegant entertaining at home is indicated. If there proves to be such a trend, that is a cue to see that the branch is prepared in linens, glassware, and even ready-to-wear. Women don't wear denims to sit at the tables they set with crystal and bone china.

The merchandising staff at the main store may see the very same straws in the wind, and draw and act upon the very same conclusions. Or they may not. A branch manager looks at local figures, and checks findings against what he knows of the local situation. It isn't necessarily identical with the over-all picture.

When Sales Fall Off

When sales in a classification fall off, it is natural for the buyer to cut back stocks and curtail promotions. There may be occasions, however, when falling sales in a branch are not, as they seem to be, an indication of waning customer interest in the classification.

In such cases, having seen the poor sales figures, the manager may want to step in and explain the causes to the merchandising division, to stave off the pruning knife. The classification may have been the victim of late deliveries, unfavorable weather, inadequate display, an all-out promotion in a competing store, or any of a number of special circumstances. If there are such extenuating circumstances, he cannot take it for granted that the buyer knows them. Even if the department manager concerned has made a report, the branch manager's own footnote to history lends added conviction.

If, on the other hand, both the figures and the facts behind them reflect shrinking demand, the classification report puts the branch on notice to get into action and see that inventory, space, staff, and promotional effort are switched from the weak classification to a more responsive one.

Learning from Others

There are times when a classification, inexplicably, does poorly at one branch but is flourishing at the main store and in other branches.

In such cases, the first step is to check on the local situation. If the classification seems to be languishing everywhere, possibly the community just doesn't care for such merchandise. If competitors are doing well with it and the branch is not, then some study of its own performance is called for.

A path to improvement may lie in studying what the competition is doing right that the branch could also do. Other branches of the same store may prove an even more fertile field to cultivate. They may have ideas about displaying and selling that have worked for them and that can be adapted to local needs.

This is not necessarily something for the branch manager to do personally, of course. But he may have to authorize a department manager to get into action along these lines, with instructions to report his findings and propose what should be done.

Correcting Stock-Sales Relationships

Typical classification reports show stock figures as well as sales, and provide a chance to inspect the stock-sales relationships. If the stock for any classification or sub-classification seems unduly high or low in relation to sales, the branch manager has every reason to interest himself in the matter.

The more branches a parent store has, the more important it is for each one individually to investigate unusual conditions of this kind. A buyer can spread himself just so thin, and then he has to depend upon the branch manager to alert him to special situations, and to pass along the ammunition for correcting them.

When stocks are light in relation to sales, lows and outs are especially likely to be present. They should be checked and reported promptly, especially if they are among basic items or others enjoying strong and continuing demand. Some stores honor requisitions for replenishments of this kind, even though the buyer has temporarily exhausted the open-to-buy. Other stores consider each request on its merits. In either case, a well documented request shows that the branch manager knows what is needed, and why.

Heavy stocks should be investigated, too, both for slow-moving items and for outs. A heavy stock is quite as likely to have holes as a light one. But it is also likely to have items that are unsuited to the branch, or that were delivered too late, or that were pushed out of sight by the branch staff and never given a chance to move. The manager's personal interest in seeing what goes on and in getting such situations corrected will help prevent their recurrence.

Investigating Markdowns

If markdowns are reported by classification, the exceptional figures in this column, too, warrant attention from the branch manager. Considering the markdown in relation to sales sheds a good deal of light on the picture. Minimal markdowns and rising sales generally mean well selected, much wanted goods. Minimal markdowns and limping sales may mean a slow-moving stock on which price adjustments are overdue.

It is important, once classification reports have pinpointed them, to analyze good as well as poor areas. Observation in a classification with a good mark-down record may produce suggestions that can be applied in other parts of the branch. Or the record may indicate a department manager of unusual ability who should be kept in mind for a bigger assignment later on.

Classifications with particularly heavy markdowns need checking on such points as poor stock arrangement, lack of interesting departmental display, poorly briefed salespeople, inadequate promotion, unbalanced assortments. Other causes: late deliveries, buying errors, careless handling of the goods, delay in getting merchandise to the selling floor once it has reached the branch.

Profit Protection

Other profit-destroyers are also brought to light by classification data, if the store supplies sufficient detail. Stock shortages, or unduly heavy expense ratios, for instance, should be investigated first and most thoroughly in those classifications that show the worst figures. Departmental data alone cannot pinpoint the trouble spots so clearly. Classification data tell you where to start.

So, if the branch manager suddenly finds himself obliged to cope with new registers, new systems, and new reports because top management has decided to compile classification data, this should not be regarded simply as an occasion for increased aspirin consumption. The beginnings may be hard, and the first billboard-like reports may be daunting, but once he learns to live with classification reports, the branch manager will find that they give him a far better idea of what his customers want and of the areas within his operation that most urgently need his personal attention.

CHAPTER 9

IMPROVING MERCHANDISING RESULTS

No merchandising operation, whether at a branch or at a main store, is so good that it cannot be made better. One mark of the good merchant is his insatiable appetite for examining results critically, in search of exploitable strengths, correctable weaknesses, and potential sources of additional volume and profit.

Not every factor in the merchandising of a branch is under the control or even under the eye of the manager. Enough of the process is within the scope of his job, however, so that it pays him to train himself and his department managers to observe, report, and in some instances, take action.

The purpose of this chapter is to outline the areas in which the branch manager is most likely to find opportunities for improvement and in which he should be most conscientious in training his department managers to be watchful and alert.

Initial Markon

Initial markon is the difference between the invoice price of merchandise (including transportation costs) and the retail price at which it is first placed in stock. Initial markon percentage is obtained by dividing the total of these differences, over a given period, by the total retail value of the goods placed in stock in that period.

The branch has little control over the factors entering into initial markon except in two ways:

1. Watching customer reaction and reporting promptly any

price that seems discouragingly high to customers, or any that seems unduly low. The faster the buyer is alerted the faster corrective action can be taken.

2. Knowing which styles or items carry a higher than usual markon, and doing everything possible to push them: displaying, suggesting, and watching stocks with particular care. The more long-markon goods the branch moves, the better the average markon percentage, and the better the profit prospects.

Markdowns

Markdowns are reductions in retail price. They are usually initiated by the buyers, and the branch staff can seldom do more than make recommendations. The manager can, however, analyze the causes of markdowns taken on branch stocks, seeking ways to avoid the repetition of preventable errors—the branch's as well as those of the merchandising staff.

Branch errors that can lead to markdowns include:

1. Careless handling, resulting in excessive damage and soilage of goods.

2. Careless housekeeping, resulting in excessive soilage.

3. "Misfiling" a good style in an inaccessible corner, or on the rack assigned to another size or price, thus slowing its sale.

4. Poor display—uninspired, uninformative, or just not enough of it.

5. Poor selling—uninterested salespeople, lack of information about the product, failure to show interest or confidence in the merchandise.

6. "Overbuying"—pressuring buyers for heavier stocks than are needed in a size, or price, or type. The temptation to do this is particularly strong with respect to merchandise for which an ad is planned.

7. Selling new stock before using up older stock of the same or similar items. The old becomes shopworn. First in, first out!

Helping the Buyer

The branch can help, too, to minimize markdowns that arise from errors and oversights of the merchandising staff, resources, or others. For instance:

1. Watching new numbers, styles, prices, size ranges, when they come into the stock. The human eye can be quicker than the electronic computer to spot a slow or fast moving number. An early report to the buyer helps:

 (a) To get rid of the slow numbers the cheapest way—by return, transfer, or a prompt markdown, and

 (b) To improve the over-all results by bringing prompt replenishments of the faster sellers.

2. Reviewing the marked down numbers visually, looking for common characteristics that appear to indicate a rejection by customers of a color, or line, or texture, or grade of merchandise. An adverse attitude, where it exists, may affect more than one department, and even more than one division. When anything of the kind is found, the branch should pass the word along promptly, to forestall future markdowns.

3. Checking incoming merchandise against the covering documents, to make sure size, style, color, etc., are exactly as specified, and that the branch is not accepting, because of a shipper's error, less salable goods than were ordered for it. This applies to inter-store transfers, as well as to receipts directly from resources. It is important to check the condition of the goods, too, so that the branch need not foot the bill, in markdowns, for soiled or damaged merchandise.

4. Paying particular attention to markdowns that appear to be caused solely by poor timing. Goods that arrive too early lose some of their bloom before the normal selling period rolls around; goods that arrive too late are no longer in demand. Passing along observations to the buyer so that better timing for branch clientele may be possible next season.

5. On merchandise received directly, checking shipments received after cancellation dates on orders. Fashion goods, especially, may no longer be salable at normal prices.

Gross Margin

Gross margin is the difference between the actual selling price of the merchandise, as rung up in the cash register, and its net cost. Profits hinge upon this figure. If it is not large enough to cover operating expenses and leave a remainder, there can be no profit.

In major and minor ways, the branch can help to keep the factors in gross margin under control. These factors include: invoice cost, incoming transportation, cash discount on purchases, markdowns, late deliveries, stock shortages, workroom costs, employee discounts, special allowances to customers.

1. Being alert to items known to have good gross margin possibilities and giving them every chance to sell.

2. Acknowledging receipt of incoming merchandise without delay. The more quickly shipments are verified and invoices are put through for payment, the less likely that the store will lose its cash discount. Many well-financed retailers find it profitable to prepay their bills and earn a further discount, called anticipation.

3. Being concerned with initial markon and markdowns, as explained previously.

4. Watching stock shortages. A special chapter discusses this problem in detail.

5. Watching alterations. If a garment requires elaborate adjustments, the chances are the store will lose money, even if it makes a substantial charge for the work. On any but normal, simple alterations, the store runs the risk of having to re-fit and re-alter the garment, or even of having the customer refuse it altogether. In men's departments particularly, one should watch the tendency of salesmen to sell a wrong size when the customer's actual size is not in stock, in the hope that the alteration department can somehow save the sale.

6. Watching employee discounts. Some employees like to share this benefit with all their friends. This is a particular hazard in suburban branches, where part-time salespeople may be friends and neighbors of customers. Occasionally, employees should be reminded that their discount percentage is actually larger than a store's total operating profit percentage, and that, although it is given cheerfully to the store family, no retail institution can afford to give it to all and sundry.

7. Watching special allowances to customers. If any department has an inordinate number of adjustments for soiled and damaged merchandise, marked down on the spot, it should be checked to see if the stock-keeping can be improved, or if allowances are being granted needlessly on goods that can be reconditioned at little or no cost.

Turnover

A good turnover figure is the result of a good operation; it means that the speed with which the merchandise in a store or department is sold and replaced is satisfactory or better. Too high a turnover may mean that the store or department is operating on dangerously narrow stocks; too low a turnover means sluggishness, and entails high carrying costs for maintaining stocks that are large in relation to sales. It often indicates a poorly selected assortment that does not sell readily.

The turnover figure is obtained by dividing net sales for a year (or other period) by the average retail inventory for that period. Figures for individual stores vary according to the size and nature of the operation.

To assist the buyers in achieving their turnover goals, the branch should do the best selling and stock-watching job of which it is capable. Every piece of merchandise unduly delayed in getting to the selling floor slows turnover. Every sale that is rung up helps raise the turnover figure; every one that is lost, pulls it down. Every piece of merchandise that overstays its welcome in stock is slowing the turnover. Every delayed transfer or delayed return to vendor slows turnover. Every fast-moving item that is sold and promptly replaced and sold again is helping to improve turnover.

Wise merchandisers think about turnover only when they are planning their season's budget and when they are reviewing past results. The rest of the time, they concentrate on keeping stocks clean and sales high, knowing that this combination is bound to result in satisfactory turnover.

The Stock You Need

An endless tug of war goes on in some store organizations between the branch, demanding more stock, and the main store merchandising staff, insisting that the branch wants more than it can sell.

A part of the problem goes back, in many cases, to the now fairly common policy of overstocking a new branch, for the sake of the impact its assortment will make upon the community. Later, when the branch is established and its customers' needs are well documented by sales experience, it can function on smaller, more accurately planned stocks. In the meantime, however, the branch personnel have become accustomed to working with lavish stocks; they need to adjust their thinking to the idea that a stock can be complete even when it is small.

For example, when a dress is about to be advertised, a branch department manager may insist that it must be present in every size and color. If this means four colors and five sizes, there will be a minimum of 20 garments added to the stock—perhaps three times what the branch is likely to sell. Six or eight garments, with the colors and sizes carefully chosen, might be adequate.

Large vs. Large Enough

There is no simple rule that specifies how large a stock should be—of a number, a classification, a department, or a branch. Constant watchfulness is needed. The better the branch knows its customers, the more accurately its staff can forecast their wants. And the less often department managers insist upon more stock

BRANCH STORE MONTHLY MERCHANDISING DIARY

Store_____   Month_____

Dept._____   Dept. Manager_____

Sales: L. Y._____   T. Y._____

1. What were your three top items this month?

_____

_____

_____

2. What classifications (customer end use) did you do the best job on?

_____

_____

3. What items do you think you could have done better with if you had had more of them to sell?

_____

_____

4. What classifications (and price-lines within classification) could you have done better with if you had had more to sell?

_____

_____

	V.G. (Very Good)	(Revised) G. (Good)	P (Poor)
5. Were your merchandise requests satisfied promptly and well?	_____	_____	_____

COMMENTS

6. Were fast selling items filled in quickly?   (YES)____(NO)____

7. Did you advise New York of slow selling items?   (YES)____(NO)____

8. Did your advising New York of slow selling items in your stock result in action?   (YES)____(NO)____

9. In your opinion were the stocks this month generally kept in proper balance by classification (end use) and price?   (YES)____(NO)____

EXHIBIT 15 (page 1)

COMMENTS   -2-

10. Was the balance between fashion merchandise
    and never-outs generally about right?   (YES)_____ (NO)_____

11. How many meetings did you hold with your salespeople as a group? _____

12. What did you talk about?

    First Week _____

    Second Week _____

    Third Week _____

    Fourth Week _____

    Fifth Week _____

                                        V.G.   G.   P
                                   (Very Good)   (Good)   (Poor)

13. How helpful were this month's "News About
    Your Merchandise" Forms?   _____   _____   _____

14. Were your special orders generally handled
    well?   (YES)_____ (NO)_____

15. Did you get answers fast enough on them to
    keep your customers satisfied?   (YES)_____ (NO)_____

16. Did you make any Tickler Card requests (where
    a saved sale might result)?   (YES)_____ (NO)_____

17. How many? _____

18. If you did, did you get good answers promptly? (YES)_____ (NO)_____

COMMENTS

This form is used by a multi-store New York City quality retail organization to
provide a monthly history of each branch store department for use by the Branch
Manager and parent store executives to effect improved merchandising performance.

EXHIBIT 15 (*page 2*)

than they can sell, the stronger their case will be when they ask for those kinds and quantities that they really need.

In the handling of staple stocks, management sometimes takes the calculated risk of planning for less than complete coverage, on the theory that a few lost sales are less costly than a too-heavy investment in stocks. Usually, the risk is taken where the customer is likely to find an acceptable substitute for the wanted item in the store's assortment.

Occasionally, however, the item on which a branch is taking a calculated risk of this kind is carried in full assortment by a nearby competitor. In such cases, the word should be passed along to management. The risk of losing customers, rather than small sales, may be a greater gamble than management wishes to take.

Managements have various ways to check on the adequacy of branch stocks. The commonest of these is to study stock and sales reports regularly. Less common, but decidedly revealing, is the requirement that each department manager of each branch file a monthly report or diary on the merchandising operation, answering such questions as "What were your best items last month?" and "What items do you think you could have done better with if you had more of them to sell?"

If a store's management does not request such information, the branch manager on his own can devise a simple form and collect such data regularly from his own department managers. It will help in locating problem spots and in knowing which areas can handle their affairs nicely without taking up his time. It will also give him the facts to document his case if he has to place a request for larger stocks, different price lines, etc., before management.

Studying Stock-Sales Reports

Increasingly, as stores computerize their stock and sales records, branch managers receive poster-sized reports containing detailed figures for all their departments and classifications. Some suggestions for coping with these reports are included in the chapter on classification data. In addition the branch manager may:

1. Check for any department or classification that had un-usually good sales in the past week (or month). Make sure the sales have been credited properly to his branch, and not mis-takenly to another. Look at the stock conditions for departments or classifications with outstanding sales to see if supplies have been replenished.

2. Check for any department or classification that shows un-usually large stock receipts in the period covered. Make sure the stock has actually been received and is not mistakenly charged to the branch. Review the promotion schedule or check with the department manager to see what selling program is planned to move any extra-heavy stocks.

3. Look for any department or classification with extremely low or high markdowns. Either condition may, but does not always, reflect a trouble spot. In the former case, unsalable goods may be cluttering up the stock instead of being reduced and moved out. In the other, poor selection, poor display, or poor stock-keeping may be indicated.

4. Personally check into any departments or classifications whose stocks or sales are unusually higher or lower than plan, in search of opportunities or problems in which it may be necessary to take a hand.

In a branch with many departments or classifications, a secre-tary or assistant can be trained to mark points of this kind in colored pencil, before the manager himself looks at the sheet. In that way, if time is limited, he can turn first to those areas that most need attention.

Building Volume

In addition to doing everything possible to build volume with the departments the branch now has, there may be opportunities to add further departments or services. Perhaps they were not needed when the unit was opened, but conditions may have created a demand for them, or other stores may be drawing trade with them, and the branch should have them.

Some of these additions may be profit services, discussed elsewhere in this book. Others may be departments or classifications already in the downtown store, but not yet in the branch. Still others may be boutiques, with merchandise drawn from two or three departments of the downtown store and concentrated in a small, special shop within the branch. A fourth possibility is merchandise to be carried in response to local needs, not necessarily felt in the downtown area.

The manager of a large specialty store's branch, discussing his own experience at an NRMA seminar, cited excellent results from a tiny beginning. In his suburb, there was no place where customers could buy distinctive artificial flowers. He set up a miniature department, served by the main store. It proved a magnet, and the traffic it drew helped other departments of the branch. Later, he added gifts and greeting cards of the "something special" type, also from main store departments. The boutique is small, powerful, and a valuable traffic builder.

Another volume-plus-traffic addition for branch stores is food service. If a branch appeared to have too little space for this purpose when it was first opened, it pays to check again with the main store's food service manager on present possibilities. Kitchen space and equipment requirements are much smaller than they were even a few years ago, now that so many convenience foods are on the market, with more coming out every year.

There may be room for a snack bar; or a present snack bar may be able to enlarge its menu and grow into a luncheon or tea room facility. Any opportunity for customers to sit, eat, rest, and refresh themselves is desirable; it is an opportunity to keep them under the branch's roof for an extra hour or two of shopping. If the need for a coffee break takes them outside the store, they may well ignore the rest of their shopping lists, or finish them elsewhere.

Local conditions may suggest further possibilities—needs that are felt in the suburban area, but not necessarily downtown. For example, local business and professional people may need a source for commercial stationery and office supplies. Inmates of nearby rest homes and homes for the aged may require clothes and shoes quite different from those wanted by young suburbanites. There may be no local camera and hobby shops; no fine candies and baked goods store; and so on. Opportunities for new departments, as well as for leased, service, and contract departments (discussed in another chapter) should be explored. Alertness and prompt action when such "no-competition" opportunities reveal themselves usually lead to added volume, traffic, and profit for the branch.

The All-Seeing Eye

Experts in merchandising often make the point that, with several branches to serve, the buyer has to lean increasingly upon systems and records, rather than upon "eyeball" control. But no one discounts the value of the trained eye in merchandising.

To improve the merchandising results in a branch, department managers should be repeatedly urged to develop trained eyes for errors and opportunities. The sloppily hung garment, the messy open-selling fixture, the low stock of children's socks—these are merchandising errors to watch for and correct. The pleased look on a customer's face, the request for an item the branch does not yet carry, the busy counter in the store across the street—these are merchandising opportunities to observe and report.

The more trained eyes the branch has at work, and the better trained they become through experience, the better its merchandising operation can be.

CHAPTER 10

SERVICES, LEASED DEPARTMENTS, AND PROFITS

Two types of departments present similar problems and similar opportunities to the branch manager: service and leased departments. In both cases, the problem is one of integrating a "different" operation into the store's image, service policies, merchandising and promotion patterns. And in both cases the opportunity is to achieve more volume, profit, and customer good will than would otherwise be possible.

Why Service Departments?

Particularly in suburban stores, service departments are giant oaks now in the process of growing out of little acorns. Profit services (or, by their older name, cost departments) function in minimum space and can run up a presentable contribution to volume and profit. More important, they can become magnets to draw traffic into the store.

Customers, especially those who live in the suburbs and who have access to cars, have formed the habit of dropping off and picking up items that need cleaning or repair. Some of their city sisters may still prefer to wait at home for pick-up and delivery, but the suburban housewife is generally eager to be on the move. She will come to a branch store for a service that she needs— and, if encouraged, will stay to spend some money in its merchandise departments.

108

Some suburban stores, particularly specialty shops, tend to shy away from services other than the traditional beauty salon and fur storage department. If the leather coats and knit dresses they sell present a cleaning problem, for example, many such retailers prefer simply to pass along to their customers the names of competent professional firms. This gesture is undoubtedly appreciated and thus a contributor to good will, but it does not have the same effect as when the store itself performs the cleaning service.

Department stores, with a wide variety of impulse items to sell, are usually more eager to install a leased operator or other functionary on their premises to handle such jobs directly for the customer. The occasion for having her dress, or draperies, or her husband's suit cleaned, or her watch repaired, can bring her back into the store and expose her once more to its merchandise. For her part, she knows that she can depend on the quality of the work, that any complaints will be heard, and that she can use her charge account to pay for it if she wishes to.

Surburban Benefits

Suburban stores, particularly those that face the competition of other nearby branches, chains, and shopping centers, make two other important points.

One is that the store or center which offers the most complete battery of services is the one to which the customer turns first when she needs something done, whether or not she has had that particular type of work done there before, or even knows for sure that it is handled there. Her first port of call is where she has already been a customer.

The second point is that, the more often the customer comes to the store, whether to buy merchandise or to drop off a repair or cleaning job, the more likely she is to come there on her next shopping expedition. Her car may not, like Dobbin, find its way without direction, but the route, the shopping center, and the store itself all become more familiar to her, and she feels at home there.

Choosing the Services

The manager's knowledge of the local situation is called into play in deciding which services his branch should offer. Whether or not he himself has the authority to add the needed service or sign up with a lessee, it pays for him to be alert to opportunities in this field. If he reports the need for a service not adequately available locally to his customers, his management may encourage him to pioneer the operation, or it may take up his suggestion for all its units.

In some instances, a branch may see advantage in offering a service, even though there is already a local facility. This would be particularly true in the case of familiar services like fur storage and watch repair, that customers normally expect to find in a department store, and that a branch almost can't afford to be without.

Another reason may be to help clinch the sale of items, usually at high unit prices, that require special cleaning or servicing— leather coats, upholstered furniture, installed carpeting, for example. Some of the customer's hesitation in buying will clear up when the salesperson can say that, when the time comes for renewing the article, the store has a department of its own to handle the work.

Among the services now offered by department stores and their branches are these:

Repair and Service: Appliance and TV, autos, cameras, china, furniture, handbags, lawn mowers, reweaving, shavers, shoes, tires, umbrellas.

Cleaning and Storage: Clothing, curtains, draperies, furs, gloves, knit garments, leather garments, rugs, shirt laundry, slipcovers, ties, upholstered furniture.

Personal: Auto rental, barber, beauty shop, bill paying, catering, check cashing, chiropodist, electrolysis, gift wrap, health aids, hearing aids, income tax preparation, insurance, library, money orders, optical, photo finishing, portrait, rentals, subscriptions, surgical supplies, theater tickets, travel, wig cleaning and styling.

Schools and Classes: Arts and crafts, bridge, cooking, dancing, driving, flower arrangement, interior decorating, investments, judo, knitting, sewing.

Vending Machines: Candy, coffee, soda, stamps.

Miscellaneous: Home improvement, contract selling, picture framing, monogramming, key making, engraving.

Many of these services require very little by way of space or investment. *Contract selling,* for example, requires only a desk from which the executive in charge works, reaching out for business from schools, hotels, motels, county institutions, nursing homes, and offices in the area. In suburban areas, the convenience of buying through a department store branch is a great attraction to purchasing agents. Opportunities for this business may be even better at the branch than in the downtown store.

Some of the services do, however, require personal involvement on the part of the branch manager or an aide. If *checks* are cashed, free or for a fee, someone in authority at the branch should keep in close touch with large employers in the area, in order to apprise them of this service, to find out when paydays are scheduled, to be informed of changes in the size of the payroll itself, and to be notified of employees whose names have been removed from the payroll.

Finding the Operator

The success of a service venture depends largely upon finding the right person or organization to operate the enterprise. Those with experience in the field stress the importance of searching until it is possible to get people who can do work of top quality. They report that customers are ready to pay a little more for a good job—much readier than they are to forgive a poor one that may have cost less.

If the operator at the branch has both know-how in his special field and a flair for merchandising and promotion, the manager will have no great problem. He may, however, have to settle for someone with skill in his specialty (the prime requirement) but no particular understanding of retailing. In that case, the branch manager or an assistant will have to play big brother to the newcomer until he learns his role in the store. If he is left to sink or swim, some of the branch's profit opportunities and good will may sink with him.

Making a Profit

When dealing with services, one expert in the field advises retailers to "Think profit, not cost." There is profit to be made on the actual sale of the service; there is profit on merchandise sales brought to the branch because the service is available under its roof; and there is profit on more productive use of the branch's space and advertising.

To keep expenses from swallowing up an undue share of the profits, stores are advised to consolidate as many services as possible at one counter or desk. Many of the services perform the actual work outside the store, and need only a clerical on the spot to check the goods in and out for them. The same staff can handle several such operations.

Consolidation also saves space and, more importantly, strengthens the impact of the service idea upon the customer. She has the convenience of being able to transact all of her repair and cleaning business in one place. If a branch dramatizes in this way the fact that it offers her a full complement of services, she will almost automatically come to it first with any mending or renewing.

Promoting Profit Services

Some services have successfully promoted themselves with little more than a listing in the store directory and a line in any appropriate merchandise advertising that the branch runs. Usually, something more is needed. The branch manager can suggest some of these forms of promotion, which have been used effectively by other services:

- Statement stuffers
- Package stuffers
- Tearoom table tents
- Giveaway book matches
- Radio spots
- Listings in classified telephone pages
- Signs in departments whose merchandise is likely to need the service
- Recommendation by salespeople who sell such merchandise
- Offers of free service to purchasers of such merchandise, such as one free dry cleaning of a man's suit purchased at the store
- Gift coupons, presented to service customers who spend a specified amount, for redemption that day in the store's merchandise departments.

Working with the Manager

The operator of a profit service and the manager of a leased department, whether service or merchandise, share a problem with the branch manager—one of liaison. The branch manager wants very much to know what the main store is planning for his unit by way of merchandise and promotion, so that he can coordinate his efforts with those of his management. The leased operators in the branch want the same sort of information from him, and for the same purpose: to do a better job.

This is true if the lessee is a one-man operation handling a minor service, or if he is manager of a large department, leased by a major millinery, or shoe, or beauty salon organization, with similar departments in hundreds of other stores throughout the country. This is true if he is brand new at retailing, or if he has generations of retail experience behind him.

The one thing that the long-experienced lessee and the beginner, the large one and the small, have in common is that they do not know, unless the manager makes a point of keeping them in touch, what goes on in the branch's own merchandise departments. And this they need to know, if they are to contribute to the store's efforts or to benefit from them. They can do both.

Establishing Liaison

The branch manager personally can set the pattern for creative liaison between his branch's own merchandise departments on the one hand and its leased departments or owned service departments on the other. Essentially, the job boils down to including the heads of these departments in all staff meetings, putting their names on the list of people to be notified about storewide events, putting them down to be told about upcoming ads, and generally treating them as all other department managers are treated.

When they know what is planned, these people can usually be counted upon for suggestions and offers of cooperation. For example, the beauty salon may offer to hair-style the models in an upcoming fashion show; the dry cleaner may offer a special price on coat cleaning concurrently with a branch coat sale; the shoe repair operator may know enough about shoes and fitting to help teach shoe salespeople; the book department manager may suggest subjects, or even help research them, when the branch manager is asked to talk to a women's club group.

And the manager can make suggestions to them.

For example, if the branch is advertising bathing suits, the beauty salon can profitably take space on the same day and on the same newspaper page to talk about summer hair styles. Each ad will gain impact from the other's presence. Similarly, if the branch runs a bridal ad, its shoe repair center may want to add a few lines about shoes dyed to match gowns, or its fine jewelry department may make a quick switch in its plans and advertise wedding bands or bridal gifts.

Such cooperation costs the branch nothing, yet it allows the lessee to adapt his advertising schedule to the store's and to use his promotion budget in ways that help both.

Living with Lessees

Leased department operators yearn to be treated as members of the family in stores where they operate departments. This attitude goes far beyond merely joining in advertising and promotion, or exchanging courtesies when there is a fashion presentation to be made to customers or selling staff.

Part of the branch manager's job is to cast an appraising eye on the way his own department managers function, and to speak out with correction or praise, as the occasion warrants. Lessees usually appreciate the same treatment, if it is offered to them.

There are two very strong reasons for responding to this need on the part of lessees. One is that, if they prosper, the branch prospers, too. The larger their volume, the larger the rent they pay to the store, since the usual arrangement is for the store to collect an agreed percentage of sales.

The other reason is that, if the leased department isn't doing quite the job it should, customers are bound to notice and be dissatisfied. So far as the customer is concerned, the department is the store's—faults and virtues alike. Any fault that is allowed to go uncorrected is paid for out of the good will the branch is trying to build up. Any fine performance that is encouraged enhances the branch's good name.

Dealing with the Supervisor

National and regional lessees usually have supervisors who visit their various installations regularly. These are people it is worth while to meet—and they appreciate a chance to talk with the head of the branch.

Like executives at the main store, the visiting supervisors cannot hope to know the branch's immediate trading area as well as its manager does. They are glad to have his personal reactions; they are glad to exchange ideas with him; they are able to tell him how problems like his own have been handled in other stores.

He may not have time to sit down with each and every one of these supervisors, but if he has a leased department that seems underdeveloped, or that doesn't quite seem to hit it off with his branch's customers, it becomes important to make the time. The supervisor's expertise in his special field, plus his home office staff's facilities, can be brought to bear upon the local problem, provided the manager points out what is disturbing him and lets it be known that he would like some action. If he does not speak out, the supervisor may not know that he is less than satisfied.

Terms of Leases

The terms of the contracts between a branch and its leased department operators have probably been worked out at the main store by top management. The branch head usually never has seen the leases, and may not know the details of their provisions. Leases are far from standardized.

The typical leased department agrees to pay the store a specified percentage of its sales, and to pay for certain of the expenses entailed in operating the department. Other expenses are met by the store. Sometimes there are provisions as to how much or how often the lessee is to advertise, who will install and repair fixtures and equipment, and so on.

These last are the points on which the manager especially needs information—the expenses that the lessee is to pay for, and any other special obligations that the lessee has assumed. Otherwise it can happen (and it has!) that the branch picks up the tab for costs that should have been charged to the lessee.

Single Standard for All

An expert on leased departments and profit services urged branch managers at an NRMA seminar: "Treat the leased departments and profit services in exactly the same manner as you treat each and every other department in your store . . . Ask yourself, 'Do I know as much about the inner workings of my beauty salon or restaurant as I do about our sportswear or children's departments?' You probably have a pretty good idea of the sales volume of your beauty salon, but when was the last time you analyzed the classification breakdown of its sales? . . . Do you know what your average sale is in the department? How many repeat customers you are serving? Which ads pull well? What the ad schedule is for the next 60 to 90 days?"

The seminar speaker was Henry Goldsmith, manager of leased and cost departments for J. C. Penney Company, Inc. He recommends assigning responsibility and authority for leased and profit services to a merchandiser of sufficient stature to assure these departments day-to-day guidance, directing the display manager to service these departments on a continuing and regular basis, and integrating promotional planning for these departments with the plans for the rest of the store.

The same authority also urges branch managers to compare their leased department performances with those of the main store, as well as with those in other branches. Exchange of figures and exchange of ideas among the branches can be beneficial, here as well as in relation to any other department. In short, his advice is to treat these departments exactly as the store's own merchandise departments are treated.

Most people who operate leased departments in department and specialty stores, and most stores that are particularly successful in their relationships with leased departments and profit services go right along with Mr. Goldsmith's thinking. In the customer's eyes, every department is part of the store. It is to the manager's interest to see that, merchandise or service, leased or owned, all departments function on as high a plane as he can help them achieve.

CHAPTER 11

MAKING BRANCH ADVERTISING PAY

Retail organizations vary widely in the degree of creative help they permit their branch manager to contribute to the promotional planning for his unit. Some give him substantial authority; some give him no more than an opportunity to listen in at planning sessions.

Wherever his own firm may stand along this scale, there is much that a branch manager can do to see that his unit gets the full benefit of any promotional outlay made for it, and to influence the direction of future outlays along lines of greatest value to sales and profits. Activities in this area fall into two main categories:

1. Making sure that every necessary step is taken to cash in on advertising run for the branch;

2. Preparing yourself to make suggestions for the future that are sound, workable, and not merely of the Oliver Twist, we-want-more type.

When Ads Are Planned

Store procedures usually set up rather elaborate channels of communication to make sure that the branch manager is advised in advance of any advertising for his unit's departments or any mentions of them in a main store ad. Equally elaborate channels are set up, too, to let the merchandising staff know whether or not the branch is prepared with stock of the goods to be advertised.

Much of the communication that reaches the branch manager's

desk also goes directly to the departments concerned. A main store buyer may be required to notify a branch department manager, perhaps 10 days in advance, that an ad is to be run. Or the advertising department may have this responsibility. Or both. Tear sheets of ads, signs, and other needed aids have their scheduled time for making an appearance at the branch.

The department manager is usually the one expected to follow through, and to notify the main store of any delay. Putting the department manager at the center of this communications web has its hazards, however. It makes small fry responsible for requiring action from buyers, advertising manager, display managers, and personnel managers who outrank them.

Some junior executives can handle these situations; some cannot. That is where the branch manager enters the picture. He should know which ones need only to have a procedure spelled out for them, and which ones need to be led by the hand and supplied moral support.

The Monthly Schedule

Customary procedure provides the branch manager with a monthly schedule of upcoming ads. This can be his lifeline. It tells him well in advance which departments will be in the news that month, and to what extent. Personally or through a dependable aide, he can then check to make sure that each department manager concerned:

1. knows that the ad is to appear, and when, and where;

2. knows what merchandise is to be featured, how much should be on hand, and when and with whom to follow up if it is not;

3. has arranged for dramatizing the goods within the department when the ad breaks;

4. knows how much extra selling help will be needed, if any, and has arranged for that help;

5. knows when to expect tear sheets of the ads, and where and when to post them;

6. knows what window or outlying displays are planned, and whom to follow up to make sure they are set up in time;

7. has scheduled and is preparing an enthusiasm-building session with the salespeople;

8. is not over-awed by any of the executives concerned and keeps at the follow-up job until results are achieved;

9. knows at what point to call upon you for reinforcement if action is slow.

Insuring Follow-Through

Some department managers need nothing much beyond this point. Others, however, may be too young, or inexperienced, or careless to be trusted to look after things on their own.

These less capable people will figure prominently on the branch manager's personal schedule of things to do as the month progresses. He should remind himself to remind them of the things they are supposed to check. If he feels that he should become involved, he is wise to avoid waiting for the zero hour. Last-ditch efforts are less likely to win the day than the timely arrival of reinforcements.

If department managers fall down on the job of following-through, and if a branch is mentioned in an ad but lacks adequate merchandise, or display, or salespeople, the branch manager is hurt in more ways than one. Customers, who couldn't care less who goofed, only know that it doesn't pay to take the store's ads seriously, and they become less responsive. Top management, when it checks the branch's figures, sees that its advertising costs were high in relation to sales. Branch profits suffer, and so does the hope of getting more promotional dollars in future.

Using the Written Word

A good deal of the communication between branch and main store and within the branch itself is necessarily over the telephone or face to face. In the matter of following through on a planned ad, however, there are times when the written word, with its record of what was said, and when, is important.

The department manager who casually tells the buyer, in the course of a conversation on several subjects, that he needs more reds for the upcoming ads, is asking to be overlooked. So is the one who tells the branch display chief over coffee that he is going to need three extra T-stands next Thursday week.

A brief memo gives the busy buyer or other executive a ready-made notation of what is needed. It also gives the department manager a carbon to use in following up. Subsequent reminders may be verbal, since there is already a written record of what has been requested. But it is a good idea to train young department managers to note on their carbons the date of each verbal follow-up, and the answer they were given.

If department managers are trained to work in this way, then if the branch head, in an emergency, has to step into the picture, he at least enters well prepared. From the department manager's notes he should be able to see what has been asked and what has been promised—much more useful than "I asked all week," or "I asked a dozen times."

Checking Results

It is to the branch manager's interest to keep a record of results on each ad and promotion—including notes of any gremlin activity that may have interfered with top performance, and also of any devices that proved especially effective. "No tear sheets posted," or "Window was stopper," speak volumes, months later, when one is trying to assess a past promotion for clues that can guide future plans.

Some organizations require reports of this kind; many more do not. A branch manager, in any case, needs the facts—first, to see for himself, and then later to point out with the help of facts what his unit requires from the central merchandising and promotion staffs for best results.

It is a mistake to assume that whatever occurred at one unit has occurred also at the main store and in other branches, and that some recording angel has noted it all down for the headquarters planners. The records at the main store are likely to tell only the highlights of the story: what was advertised, at what cost, and with what sales results.

Qualifying details do not always get on the record. But the people right on the scene can observe and note down such points as, for example, that a local store had the same item that day at cut price. Or that the branch had many try-ons but few sales, indicating perhaps that the fit was poor, and that sales would have been better if the garment had not proved disappointing to customers.

ADVERTISING RESULTS REPORT

Date _____

Medium _____   Store _____

Date of Ad _____   Department _____

Weather _____   Dep't Manager _____

ITEM	Price		Amount on hand	No. Sold Each Day						COMMENT
	Adv.	Reg.		M	T	W	T	F	S	

Reporting Advertising Results--A simple form like this one summarizes results of individual ads--sellouts, continued response, indifference, or whatever the case may be. Study of several such reports provides clues to merchandise, prices, media, that are most effective for branch.

EXHIBIT 16

Other possibilities: Customers may have looked over the advertised goods and asked for something better or something less expensive. Indication that the price line or quality was wrong for the branch! Or color, style, or fabric, may have failed to please. An ad can draw customers, but it cannot make sales if the merchandise itself is unappealing.

Occasionally, an ad is so right for a branch that the manager feels it would be wise to repeat it, to strike again while the iron is still hot. When that happens, the facts, figures, and recommendation should be set before the sales promotion manager and buyer promptly. If the branch manager moves quickly enough, the merchandise to back up a second ad in his unit's behalf may be on hand at the main store or readily available from the resource.

Using the Record

Some information on results gets back to buyers and merchandise managers at the main store in conversations or memos at the time of the promotion involved. That doesn't relieve the branch, however, of the need for its own record, even if that record is nothing more elaborate than marginal notes on the manager's copy of the monthly advertising schedule.

As he reviews his notes from time to time, the branch manager finds himself developing a fairly clear picture of the kinds of merchandise offerings and ads that are most effective at his branch. He will also see that some buyers seem to do a better job than others of anticipating response. From the successes, he may be able to develop conclusions as to how to minimize failures in future.

These conclusions, and the facts to support them, will come in handy next season or next year, when plans are being made for the branch's advertising and promotion. Details of what happened on previous occasions will have grown dim in the minds of the planners, by that time. The branch manager who comes to a planning session with significant facts on past experience at his fingertips will simply be "gittin' thar fustest with the mostest."

It pays!

How Promotion Is Planned

Promotional planning begins with facts.

When the merchandising and promotion divisions start work on the plans for a department, the first step is to assemble facts about the previous year's experience. These include such points as:

1. The ads and events of the previous year.
2. The sales results achieved by each.
3. The important events of major competitors in the previous year.
4. The cost of last year's efforts, both in dollars and as a percentage of net sales.
5. The most and least productive of last year's individual ads and events.

Against this background, plans for the current year are drawn up. The common tendency is to seek to repeat what produced best response last year, and to avoid anything resembling the failures, unless there are qualifying circumstances to be considered. Here is where the branch's notes on the story behind last year's figures become a valuable footnote.

Making Suggestions

When a branch manager offers suggestions or asks for some change of emphasis in the promotions planned for his branch, he is more likely to win his point if he presents facts and arguments in terms of the principles on which merchandising and promotion executives themselves plan.

For example:

1. *Play the winner; move from strength.*

A branch may have a uniquely favorable climate for a classification or price line that is having something less than its own way in other store units. In asking for promotion of that merchandise, it is important to bring out the relevant facts—for example, that there is no real competition locally for the grade or item concerned, and that the branch has a wide-open field to exploit.

2. *Advertising should be largely restricted to proven sellers.*

If there is special pleading to be done for a department, or classification, or price line that has been languishing at a branch, and if there is nothing more to support the request than that the merchandise "needs" advertising, the plea will probably be turned down.

There are several reasons why this is so. One is that, if customers are cold to the merchandise without advertising, they are not likely to develop a fondness for it through advertising alone. Something about the goods may be less than right.

Another reason is that, if advertising is invested in goods with natural acceptance among the store's customers, sales and profits are bigger in relation to promotional costs than if the advertising is swimming against the tide.

A third, and possibly the most important reason, is that if advertising concentrates on what people *don't* want, the branch presents an image to its community of having unsuitable merchandise. If it offers mostly what they do want, the branch presents itself as a place that can be counted on to have what people like.

3. *Successes, not mistakes, should be repeated.*

If the branch had a success because of special local conditions that still hold true, its manager is on firm ground in asking for a repeat, even if other branches were less successful with the same offering. Conversely, if the others did well with merchandise or with an approach that left the branch's community cold, its manager has reason to ask to be excused from participating in any planned repeats.

4. *Profitable items should be promoted in the majority cases.*

Before urging special attention to an item, or classification, or department, it is well to look into its profit possibilities as far as one is able. Stores much prefer to put promotional money behind merchandise that earns a profit for them. "And we get a good markon," can be the clinching argument.

5. *All advertising should have a purpose.*

In fact, a good ad generally serves more than one purpose. It sells merchandise and it reinforces the store's image as a fashion leader. Or it clears end-of-season stock and reinforces the store's claim as a haven for bargain hunters. Or it sells one item and attracts traffic that will bring customers and sales all through the store.

Before suggesting an ad or an event for a branch, the manager should think of all the purposes it can serve and play up those that are most important to the branch's present and future success —dominance, fashion image, or whatever it may be. A good ad sells only one idea, but that idea can often serve more than one purpose.

6. *Waste Not, Want Not*

Not every idea a manager puts forth in behalf of his branch will be accepted. In case of a turndown, he can do as some of the country's most creative advertising executives do: save it! If the idea is good, its day will come.

Other Ways to Help

If a branch's area is served by newspapers and other media not seen or heard in the main store's city, it should not be taken for granted that someone at headquarters is observing the local ads as closely as the branch executives do.

Wise branch managers call the newspapers of their communities and report any errors in print or positioning of their own ads, so that the store does not pay (and charge the branch) for more than was actually received. They also watch ads of other stores in these local media and clip any that they think the advertising department should see. It's quicker than writing up a memo, and surer than passing the word along verbally.

If store policy allows the use of in-store handouts, observation at the entrances can reveal a good deal about customer reaction to the offerings—sometimes more than sales figures alone can indicate. Comments and suggestions from the branch manager can help the sales promotion staff choose for his unit's handouts those merchandise items that are most likely to succeed.

If telephone orders are handled directly by the branch, personal checks on the telephone service are a good investment. One purpose, of course, is to find and correct any slow, rude, or careless handling of customer calls. Another purpose is to spot those occasions when an ad pulls such excellent telephone response that the switchboard cannot handle all the calls. When customers get busy signals for hours, their willingness to buy an advertised item may be greater than its sales alone will show. The advertising department should be told, so that it knows its own strength in the area of winning response. And, if the busy-all-morning situation happens often, something should be done about adding trunk lines or otherwise improving the handling of telephone orders.

Willingness to help the promotion department keep in touch pays off in many ways. But especially does it pay off in giving the advertising staff the "feel" of a branch and its environment. Once they have this, they can do an increasingly better job for it. And that's what every branch manager wants.

CHAPTER 12

BUILDING SALES THROUGH
MERCHANDISE DISPLAY

One of the most effective and least expensive selling tools available to retailers is good display. Department and specialty stores are masters of the medium, but they cannot afford to be complacent, especially in their branches. Other forms of retailing, from giant chains to tiny Momma-Poppa stores, are using the very same tool, and with ever-increasing skill. Many such stores rub shoulders with the branch and compete with it for the consumer's attention.

The typical branch has a display man or crew assigned to it. In addition to the skills he brings to the job, he has the guidance of the display director at the main store, who plans major presentations, works out the display budget, and provides equipment, supplies, and accessories. The buyers at the main store, too, lend a hand. On their visits to branch departments, they are usually expected by management to check on merchandise presentation in their respective departments and suggest any improvements that may be needed.

With all these experts at work, there is nevertheless a great deal for the manager to do to reinforce their efforts and add selling impact to the branch's visual presentations.

What Display Includes

One of the first steps toward getting good display in the branch is to make department managers and salespeople aware that everything the customer sees is part of the merchandise display package. If they do not realize this, they can balk even the best-planned efforts to move merchandise.

For example, it is not at all unusual to find a high-fashion store spending a fortune in advertising to project itself as a fashion leader—only to have its departments prominently featuring racks of leftovers, conspicuously labeled, "Reduced for Clearance." The clearance rack has its place in almost any department, but when it is permitted to dominate, it creates a bargain atmosphere, instead of a fashion image.

The same sort of thing happens in infants' departments, where layette salesgirls don white uniforms to emphasize that everything for the infant is immaculate and sanitary, but allow self-selection racks at or near the counter to become messy.

What Display Can Do

Merchandise display can accomplish many ends. Among these are:

- reflect the character the store or department wishes to reflect
- set a mood for a season or an event
- dramatize a fashion trend
- highlight new and distinctive items
- create the effect of a boutique
- feature best sellers or potential best sellers
- feature high-profit items
- tie in with a store ad, a manufacturer's ad, or a magazine feature
- tell the story of a product
- show products as they are in use
- dramatize the breadth of your assortment
- encourage the purchase of related merchandise
- encourage the purchase of more than one of an item
- encourage (or discourage) self-selection.

Making the Staff Display-Conscious

Reviewing with department managers the purposes that merchandise display can serve as one means of making them more display-conscious than they are. Occasional round-tables on how to accomplish various ends may stimulate their thinking and bring about a healthy exchange of ideas—and perhaps some tonic criticism.

If sessions of this kind do nothing more than to get department managers in the habit of repeatedly checking the appearance of their respective areas, they will have accomplished a lot. Presumably, every display and rack and fixture in the store is someone's responsibility, and is dusted and straightened each morning. But the typical branch department has to live through a long day of active customer traffic. Merchandise becomes disarranged, signs disappear, bins and racks show empty spots. It should be everybody's job to note and correct these conditions as fast as they occur.

Making department managers aware of the value of neat, attractive displays is an important step toward making the entire staff appearance-conscious. The branch manager's own comments, approving or otherwise, as he passes through the store, can also help. A pleasant acknowledgment, when he sees a salesgirl straightening up the merchandise during a lull, will usually pay dividends.

Working with the Professional

Ideally, a good retail display man is a merchant as well as a professional in his own field. If the branch is fortunate enough to have such a man assigned to it, the principal problem will be feeding him the information he demands so that he can create windows and interior displays that really sell.

Actually, the man assigned to the branch may not yet be quite so self-sufficient. He may not know what to ask, or how to reach the person who can give him the necessary facts. Without them, he may produce windows that are artistically satisfying, but not exactly loaded with sales power in terms of that branch's merchandise and its customers.

Such waste can be prevented by setting up machinery for supplying him with information. If the store has no regular procedure for doing this, the branch manager might work up a form like those used in requesting advertising. The display man's needs are a little broader than those of the copywriter, however, since he may have to select or devise special props or show related merchandise.

For a starter, here are some points such a form should cover:

• the objective; what the display is expected to accomplish.
• the story of the merchandise: fashion, use, selling points, available sizes, colors, materials, price, etc.
• interesting background information about the merchandise, if any: foreign origin, perhaps, or new scientific achievement, or whatever it may be.
• related items that are used or worn with the merchandise, and the location of the departments that sell such merchandise.
• tie-ins, if any, with store or resource advertising, magazine mentions, etc.

In addition to what is supplied him for individual projects, the display man also needs merchandise information of a more general type—about fashion trends, the store's merchandising aims, incoming merchandise, planned events, for instance. If there is no other mechanism for keeping him informed (and even if there is!), it is a good idea to invite him to as many divisional or storewide briefings as he can attend. He probably won't have time for many sessions at the departmental level, but if any department has special problems or exceptional growth opportunities, he should make a point of sitting in at its meetings as often as possible. Helpful suggestions may develop.

The activities of local competition mean as much to him as they do to the merchandising and advertising staff. If he does not have time to look around with any great regularity himself, department managers and others who visit competing stores should report to him whenever they see something exceptional. The more he knows about the branch and its neighbors, and the more the merchandise people are aware of the ways in which he can help, the more he can do for the branch.

Working with Non-Professionals

Many, possibly most of the displays at a branch are made by people with no professional training for the job. Yet these are the displays and stock arrangements that greet the customer right at the point of sale—the ones that are set up by department managers and salespeople.

Lacking training in display techniques, salespeople and their supervisors may never think of new or better ways to show the merchandise. Bath towels may continue to be set up in stacks, because no one has suggested fanning out a rainbow assortment to dramatize the wide range of colors. Scarfs may continue to be set out folded, in neat, overlapping rows, because no one has suggested that a particular size, color, or kind should be shown opened and draped, to emphasize that it is fashion's darling at the moment. Dresses, sportswear, and men's suits may be hung by size, with little or no effort to arrange the garments within each size in some sort of color range, because no one has suggested that this set-up can make the overall effect more attractive.

To get better displays from the many non-professionals whose fingers are in the merchandise presentation pie, the branch manager may have to hold meetings, run contests, invite some departments to study and judge the work of others, and in general, get his people more display-conscious. A good deal of potential talent may reveal itself in the lower echelons, if he digs for it. Among the part-timers, especially, he may find housewives who have had art training, or whose interior decorating efforts in their own homes have sharpened their sense of what goes with what.

If the display head at the branch, or the display manager at the parent store, is agreeable and articulate, it is a good idea to ask for a talk or demonstration of display principles at the branch. His efforts may not bring the branch's people into the professional class overnight, but they will undoubtedly increase everyone's awareness of the possibilities in display—and everyone's appreciation of the job the experts achieve, week in and week out, in the store's windows and feature displays.

Providing the Props

Research has demonstrated quite pointedly that props for display can be worth their weight in sales, particularly if they make it easier for the customer to visualize the merchandise in use. If a branch is poorly equipped, the manager may have to add his voice to that of the branch display executive in order to get what is needed.

It is important to remember, however, that one unit's needs are not necessarily identical with those of others—nor is its storage space. If a branch is cramped for room, it may be wiser to forego the purchase of props that are bulky or lacking in versatility and to use ingenuity instead.

Branches, in some instances, have insisted upon manikins for apparel display, only to find that garments for special promotions arrived in the wrong sizes for the figures, or that children hurtled into the standing figures with damage to themselves and the display.

There are alternatives: Ledge displays (provided they don't block the view) that are out of the reach of children. T-stands, that can be set up anywhere and used for any size. Manikins and displays can also go on top of racks, be suspended from ceilings, or mounted on columns.

The All-Important Sign

In many stores (not just branches), there is a tendency to forget what is perhaps the single most important selling element in any merchandise display: the sign. If the display has enough interest for the customer to get her to pause and look, the sign should be there to complete the selling job—especially if there is any possibility that a salesperson will not be at her elbow to wait on her the moment she stops.

Some retailers feel that a sign is adequate if it carries the price and includes also some generic terms, like "dresses" or "men's slacks." Those who really use display fully insist upon more than that. They like their signs to tell the story of the merchandise: "Cool, comfortable A-line dresses," or "Rugged slacks for active boys."

Usually, directional signing is adequate in a modern store. The customer can see easily where to go for under- or outerwear, where to find housewares or bedspreads. But when she gets to the department in which she expects to make a purchase, she often finds featured merchandise in a special display or on a special rack, with nothing to tell her why it deserves the attention. With a strong, selling sign, the same display can motivate her to buy.

Signs are a vital part of display. If yours have to be ordered from a central sign shop, remind your department heads as well as your display man to get the requests in early and to follow up as systematically as they do for deliveries of advertised merchandise. Even if they are made at the branch, some lead time is still needed to do the work in an orderly way.

When merchandise is advertised, copies of the ad should be placed in the department, as well as in other places (elevators, stair landings, etc.) designated for posting of store ads. This may be the responsibility of the department manager concerned, but the branch manager and the branch display man should also make a habit of checking to see that it has been done, along with the setting up of banners, poster-type announcements of special sales, and any other in-store advertising. Both should train themselves, too, to see that such signs are removed the moment their day is over. Yesterday's events have no place on today's bulletin board. Neither is there any reason to continue to post signs about reduced prices when the special sale is over and the merchandise has been marked up again to its normal retail price.

A point to check relentlessly is the cleanliness and completeness of signs in self-service areas. Size and price designations sometimes are lost; or they become dirty or torn. In such condition, they are of little help to the customer and reflect no credit on the branch. Department managers and salespeople, as well as the display man and the branch manager, should train themselves to watch for signs that need replacement.

The Boutique Effect

Large stores have found it increasingly effective to set up special shops or boutiques, complete with their own special sales-girls and special stock, each catering to some distinct need or class of customer.

Branch stores, with limited space and thin stocks, and without enough salespeople to make such specialization feasible, are likely to find the boutique *effect* better suited to their needs. Using ingenuity rather than engineering, the effect of a shop is created—and just as readily eradicated to make room for a newer idea.

One of the simplest devices is to throw a spotlight on a section of wall in or near a particular department—linens, men's sportswear, dresses, or what have you. The wall may be painted in a bright color or in stark white. Garments can be hung against it from hooks; accessories to go with them can be shown on shelves attached to the wall, or hanging from hooks. Linens and towels can be shown on shelves, with one or two pieces opened and draped against the wall. Travel or celebrity posters, an appropriate name, or any other "atmosphere" touch can be added.

If department managers and display crew work out boutique effects with color, light, and portable fixtures, they can set up and dismantle shops according to current needs, and at minimum expense.

In developing boutique effects, a branch may not be able to get a great deal of help from its main store, whose executives are used to working with larger areas, heavier stocks, and more varied customer traffic than exist at the branch. Managers of the store's other branches may have ideas, however. Other sources would include: fixture manufacturers; merchandise resources; consumer magazines; a tour of the branch's shopping center and others within reach.

Making Use of What You Have

One branch manager says: "The most important thing we do in the branch is take the customer's money." This is one job that display alone cannot do. The salespeople have to join forces with the visual merchandising at this point. To do this effectively, they need to know not only what is in the windows, but also what is special about that merchandise—and about any merchandise highlighted within the department.

In theory, all this information is duly passed along to them by the department managers. It is wise to check, however, by chatting with an occasional salesperson and asking for an opinion about a display, or a report of customer reaction to it. Whether or not any useful ideas develop from such conversation, they will at least underscore the branch manager's interest in getting effective displays.

Also important is the matter of noting results, particularly good results. If a display seems to be doing an excellent job of attracting customers, and if it is a temporary installation, like a window or featured interior display, it is advisable to photograph it and record its achievements on the back of the picture.

With a gallery of winners to study, and perhaps a companion gallery of non-starters, branch manager and branch display man may be able to find common factors in the merchandise or the method to guide future efforts.

Sources of Ideas

Display people, being creative, are constantly on the lookout for new ideas, which they then translate into effective displays for the stores in which they work. Many sources for display ideas are not readily available to the branch's display man, although they are likely to cross the desks of the branch manager and his merchandising staff. Among these are the advertising and editorial pages of buyer publications; the illustrations in consumer fashion and shelter magazines; promotion portfolios supplied by publications and merchandise resources.

To clip these items and pass them along to the display man with a tactful "Of interest?" is a helpful habit to form. Similarly, a description or sketch of singularly effective displays seen in other stores can be passed along. Wise procedure is simply to route the material to the display person, and to avoid implying that an exact copy of someone else's work is wanted. If an idea strikes a spark, the display man may express it in ways that bear little surface resemblance to the original, but that are well suited to the branch's purposes.

Display, like advertising, is one of a retailer's vital lines of communication. Anything that helps a branch use it more effectively in reaching customers is a step in the right direction.

CHAPTER 13

MAKING CREDIT WORK FOR THE BRANCH

Credit is one of the most important customer services a branch can offer. Experience has demonstrated that the charge account is a powerful magnet for drawing customers into a store and for enhancing the pull of its advertising.

Credit, however, is no longer exclusively a department store service. Other forms of retailing offer it; banks offer it; service organizations offer it. Almost any type of seller today can build a credit link between himself and his customers.

A branch store, nevertheless, has special advantages in this field. It has the very considerable experience and know-how of the main store's credit manager to draw upon, and it has its own branch manager on the local scene, to alert the credit office to whatever problems or opportunities develop there. The combination can put the branch far ahead of its competition in the creative use of this particular customer service.

Charge Accounts

Customers have reported that they like department store charge accounts for convenience features—freedom from carrying cash, ease of telephone and mail shopping, relief from staying home to wait for C.O.D.'s.

They like also the prestige of a charge account. It recognizes them as regular customers; it provides ready identification; it brings advance notice of special sales. Young families have a special appreciation of the charge account as a means of establishing their credit rating—a point that has particular significance for the suburban branch, whose customers are largely drawn from just this group.

Studies of customer habits have shown that the woman with a charge account at a store is more likely to see its ads than those of other stores with which she has no account. They also show that she is more likely to shop where she has an account before going to other stores, and that there is a better than even chance that she will make a purchase in the course of her visit.

When a customer has several charge accounts, the impact of each one upon her shopping habits is lessened. But, even when she has several, those stores where she has accounts retain a better chance of selling her than those where she has none.

Community charge plates, bank charge plates, and similar group credit facilities do not create a close relationship with any one store and do not give any of the subscribing stores an advantage similar to what the branch enjoys when it has the customer on its charge roster.

Soliciting Charge Customers

Soliciting charge customers is a continuous process. Initially, solicitation is usually done on a broad scale in a branch's area, months before the unit is opened. Yet, no matter how many accounts were on the books on opening day, or are on the books today, there is an ever-present need to add new ones.

Families move out of the branch's neighborhood, or out of its income bracket; their accounts fall idle and must be replaced by new ones. New people come into the community and, if they are not encouraged to open accounts, they may establish credit elsewhere and give other stores that important first chance to serve them.

The manner and frequency of general charge account solicitation campaigns are usually matters for the store's credit manager to decide, but there is room here for collaboration. The branch manager is in a position to insist upon complete cooperation from the staff of his unit and to educate them to the importance of a large and active charge account roster. He is also in a position to pass along to the credit manager word of any local conditions that could affect the timing or nature of his campaigns. Some of the relevant activities of other stores in the area, plans for new residential constructions, rumors of plant openings or shutdowns, for instance, could conceivably escape his attention, but could scarcely escape that of an alert branch manager.

Using the Salespeople

One of the most effective weapons in the account-opening arsenal is the salesperson, since she has an opportunity to suggest a charge account each time she rings up a cash sale. Many stores have a standing policy of offering a small cash bonus for each active account opened as a result of a salesperson's suggestion. Others do this only during special campaigns. Still others find that their customers resent pressure of this kind, and therefore instruct their people to wait for the customer to take the initiative.

If customer reaction is different at a branch than it is downtown or at other branches, the manager should discuss this with the parent store's credit manager. Change in procedure may be possible to take advantage of whatever special circumstances apply.

The branch manager can help make his salespeople more effective in selling credit by talking to them (or having the department managers talk to them) about how a timely suggestion of credit can clinch a sale and be a real service to the customer. There are often occasions when the customer indicates that she would like to buy a related item, or take advantage of a special sale, but does not have cash readily available. There are also occasions when an item is out of stock or must be ordered specially for the customer, and no exact delivery date can be promised. The suggestion of a COD in such cases is simply the suggestion of an added inconvenience to the cash customer; the offer of a charge account opens up a new area of service.

No matter how convincingly the case for inviting customers to open charge accounts is presented to the salespeople, however, enthusiasm will flag in time, and will need booster shots. Particularly before the heavy buying seasons, like Easter, back-to-school, and Christmas, it is a good idea to talk to salespeople and department managers on this subject.

The fountainhead of enthusiasm for opening accounts is, of course, the credit manager himself. If invited, he will probably be glad to speak to branch salespeople about how credit helps them to help their customers, and to department managers about how credit helps them to build volume and profits.

Silent Campaigners

In addition to what the salespeople do to encourage charge accounts, there are a number of silent compaigners a branch can employ, with the credit manager's approval. One is the desk at which the customer finds blank application forms, together with a box into which to drop the completed form. Such desks can be placed almost anywhere in the store—from the credit office itself, for the convenience of people in a hurry, to the front door. They have even been seen in use in mid-winter, outside the door of a suburban branch.

Windows and departmental displays, from time to time, can carry a reminder of your credit facilities. With any items that represent a long-considered purchase, the offer of credit may be just what the customer needs to get her inside the door. The same thing is true, also, of many small items that are bought on impulse. The convenience of credit makes itself very plain to the customer when an inadequate supply of cash balks her desire to buy something she wants and can afford.

There are many other opportunities to remind customers that charge accounts simplify shopping and that the branch can take applications for them. These opportunities would include, of course, any ads that may be run for the branch itself, in newspapers, or on radio or television. Also, tea-room table tents, elevator cards, dressing room cards, and even, sometimes, the talks that the manager himself gives to consumer groups.

The end result of continued effort is more names on the charge account list, more people who receive catalogues and statement stuffers from the store, more people who have a special interest in the branch and feel that they belong there.

Establishing Accounts

If the branch has a credit office of its own, to which customers come to be interviewed about opening accounts or to discuss problems arising from their accounts, this office should be as pleasant and friendly as the branch manager can make it. A bad impression upon the customer at this point, when she is ready to link herself to the store with a charge account, can nullify all the good work that has been invested in promoting credit.

It is wise to check the physical appearance of the credit office regularly, of course, or have a dependable aide do that. This is an area where something more than just good housekeeping can be desirable. Home-like touches, such as flowers on desks, and pictures on walls, help to put the customer at her ease and dispel any embarrassment she may feel at discussing her income and financial affairs with a stranger.

When a new branch is opened, any credit interviewers assigned there are generally trained at the main store. As the original branch credit staff expands or is replaced, this practice of providing training at the main store may fall into the discard and the branch interviewers themselves may train their assistants or successors.

If, for this or any other reason, the level of service is dropping off from what the store's customers have a right to expect, the credit manager can help. He can call the branch credit people in to the main store for refresher training, or send someone to the branch for that purpose. The one thing he cannot do, however, is make a day-to-day check on how the interviewers are handling customers. That's for the branch manager and his aides to do.

Occasionally, the credit office takes what appears to be a long time in approving or rejecting a customer's application. Some

branch managers, therefore, feel they should have more autonomy in this area, so that they can give the customer a speedy
"Yes" or "No." Consumer credit, however, is a highly specialized
field, in which decisions require carefully developed skills and
much up-to-the-minute information. Since the account on which
the answer is delayed longest may be the very one on which decision is trickiest, wise policy is to assure the customer that the
branch will follow up, and do that—but no more.

Authorizing Credit Sales

A store opening its first branch sometimes provides it with a
list of accounts in good standing, or with a negative list of those
that should be questioned, and permits it to authorize its own
credit sales. Later, as additional branches are opened, or as improved communications equipment becomes available, the same
store may withdraw that responsibility and require all credit sales
to be authorized centrally. Among the stores participating in the
surveys that guided this book, 94 per cent say they authorize
credit centrally. This figure includes reports from some with but
a single branch, and also from some with branches 50 miles or
more distant.

The key to efficient handling of credit authorization is to make
sure that everyone knows his part in the routine. This means that
each salesperson should know the floor limits in every department
in which she may be called upon to ring up a sale. If these limits
can be posted at the register, beyond the customer's line of vision,
that is one possibility of avoiding error. The back of the salesbook
is another spot for such reminders. So is the stockroom, particularly in departments where a large portion of the merchandise is
kept behind the scenes.

Authorization procedure should be taught and re-taught, especially in branches that use many part-time and temporary salespeople. If specific telephones are set aside for this purpose, the
authorization routine should be posted near them, so that even the
newest member of the staff will know what to do.

Also important to teach and re-teach: What to do about various special situations, such as when the customer reports a change of address while making her purchase, or when she doesn't have her charge plate with her. A shopping tour of a fairly large branch may reveal variation in the way individual salesgirls handle such customers. It has been known to happen that a customer will be permitted to make her purchase without plate in one department, but will be required by another to secure a shopping pass, with no explanation being offered in either case.

Special Situations

Important also is the matter of training salespeople in how to talk to a customer whose credit appears to be questioned. It is a natural but mistaken tendency to assume that anyone who is asked to call at the credit office before charging her next purchase is a defaulter. If such a request is relayed to the customer in the tone of voice that teachers reserve for sending an unruly pupil to the principal's office, a lot of the branch's hard-won good will may go right down the drain. Pleasant, neutral attitudes are safest.

This is true also, when there are overdue accounts on which the store must press for collection, or when there are overbought customers who should be asked to cut back their purchases. Situations of this kind can be delicate in the extreme, and are best handled by professionals who know how to avoid the pitfalls. Branch personnel, unless they are specially trained and authorized by the credit department, will find it wise simply to refer the customer to the credit office, which has all the facts, and to decline to enter into discussion.

There may be times, however, when the branch has some background information about an individual customer that should be considered, and that may not be readily available to the credit manager. In such cases, the branch executive should pass the facts along, but avoid making any commitment to the customer directly. This procedure is sound, also, when there are credit adjustments to be made or any other situations that require the expert's touch.

Efforts in the area of credit will pay off most handsomely and involve the branch manager and his store in the least difficulty if the branch staff will concentrate on interesting customers in opening and using their accounts, but leave the management of those accounts to colleagues who have the special combination of knowledge, skills, and intuition that are found in good credit managers.

CHAPTER 14

GETTING MAXIMUM SALES PRODUCTIVITY

The largest item of expense in a branch store is its payroll, and the largest element of the payroll itself is selling salaries. In order to get maximum productivity from each selling payroll dollar, the branch manager should interest himself in:

· seeing that the best salespeople available are hired,
· seeing that they are trained well, not only in system and salesmanship, but also in merchandise information,
· budgeting manpower requirements to maintain adequate coverage without overstaffing,
· avoiding waste in the way that salespeople's time is used.

Practical suggestions for achieving these objectives have been culled from the experience of many retailers and are compiled in this and the two subsequent chapters.

The Hiring Process

Employment activities are usually handled for the branch by a personnel executive assigned to it, or working in its behalf at the main store. If hiring is done at the branch, policies and procedures are laid down by the main store's personnel director. But that official is seldom able to drop in at the branch and check on performance. This becomes a task for the branch manager. If he makes a point of observing hiring interviews at unannounced intervals, he may sometimes find conditions that require correction. Some of these, like unpleasant physical surroundings, he may be able to correct on his own. Others, like inept interviewing, he can refer to the main store. If he allows the initial contact with the store, the employment interview, to make a bad impression upon applicants, the branch's chances of recruiting pleasant, capable people will be poor indeed.

Finding Applicants

In order to make sound selections, the employment office needs a pool of good applicants from among whom to choose. The branch manager, knowing his community as he does, may be able to guide the employment supervisor to the best places in which to ask or advertise for help—local shopping news, radio, the employee bulletin board, schools, or whatever the case may be. The situation in the branch's community is not necessarily identical with that encountered in hiring for the main store or for other branches.

The branch manager's public relations work can pay dividends in this area by attracting acceptable people to his store for temporary or permanent jobs. A flow of desirable applicants is one of the by-products of the hours he spends publicizing his branch among schools, youth groups, women's clubs, and other community organizations.

One branch manager provided an excellent example on how good public relations help. His personnel executive was desperate for temporary, part-time people before Christmas, but all the usual channels produced little response. The branch, however, had an active consumer advisory group, with whom the manager met regularly. The members were club women—outgoing, joiner types who knew everyone in town. A personal SOS went from the manager to the ladies—and in no time at all, they turned up enough applicants to meet the emergency and provide a reserve list for future needs.

Reporting Back

The employment office cannot do its best work in an ivory tower. If supervisors do not report back on the quality of the help supplied to them, the employment office has no way of knowing whether or not it has been using the right criteria in selecting people, and whether or not its preliminary system training has been effective.

The branch manager can encourage such reporting in any of a number of ways. Among them:

• Require employment office to send a written request to each supervisor for a report on each new employee after a designated number of days on the job.

• Require a similar check to be made with each new employee.

• Circulate personally in the store and spot-check on the degree of satisfaction among supervisors and new employees.

• Impress upon supervisors and employment office that the prime purpose of such checks is to assist the employment office in its future work in their behalf.

During peak hiring periods, such follow-up and reporting may have to be suspended. That is all the more reason to insist upon a conscientious effort during relatively slow periods, so that, by the time peaks come along, the employment office has good rapport with the department heads and is functioning with a sure hand.

Basic System Training

The methods and procedures used for basic system training at the main store are not always ideally suited to a branch. The main store, for instance, may have excellent facilities for classroom teaching and may process new employees in sufficient numbers to make this approach the practical one to follow. A branch, however, may not even have a classroom, and may not hire enough people at one time, ordinarily, to make classroom work feasible. In some instances, personal conferences, programmed instruction, and self-study leaflets may constitute the practical approach.

The branch manager should know how teaching is done in his unit, and with what success. He can check by dropping in on a training session, and by spot checking among new salespeople and their supervisors. If he has reason to be less than satisfied, he should discuss the problem with the branch's training executive, the training director at the main store, or both. If he provides these experts with a documented report of successes or failures he has found, they can adjust their approach to his branch's needs.

Basic Merchandise Training

Branches, like their parent stores, usually rely upon a combination of the sponsor and the buyer to educate a new salesperson about the merchandise. In the branch, there are also department managers to assist in the education process.

In many branches, however, buyers' visits are few and hurried; department managers supervise several classifications of merchandise, and salespeople are far less narrowly specialized than those at a downtown store. They need more merchandise training than those at the main store, but are less likely to get it unless the branch itself takes steps to help them. Among the steps that can be taken are:

• Develop a reference library of basic merchandise information on broad subjects like fabrics, clothing construction, color, home furnishings, etc., from which the training director can develop or help department managers develop talks, leaflets, and exhibits for salespeople. Sources include schools, libraries, and museums, as well as merchandise resources and buyers.

• Teach department managers to teach. The training director can instruct them in methods of presenting information and conducting meetings.

• Invite buyers to send merchandise information along in any form that is easiest for them, promising that someone of the branch will see that it is used. Accept graciously and be prepared to work with anything from a hand-written memo to a tape-recorded talk.

• When an important talk is to be given to branch salespeople, beg or borrow a tape recorder and use the playback or excerpts from it to reach those who missed the occasion. Transcribe appropriate parts for the branch's reference library of merchandise information.

• Consider storewide or divisional meetings, contests, quizzes, on fundamental merchandise information needed in more than one department.

- Maintain merchandise information bulletin boards in employee lounge, cafeteria, locker area. Post leaflets, clippings, even good informative merchandise labels. Use advertising and editorial material in daily paper, women's and men's fashion magazines, and trade publications as sources. Invite salespeople also to submit material.

- In departments to which manufacturers supply demonstrators, either regularly or occasionally, invite these men and women to talk to the store's own employees on merchandise and on sales techniques. These are usually highly trained, very articulate people who can do a good job. They should be asked, however, to refrain from pushing their own lines exclusively in talks to store employees.

Enthusiasm is contagious. The initiative and eagerness demonstrated by the branch in its quest for basic merchandise information encourages the cooperation of buyers and resources.

Branch Training Facilities

Some branches have excellent training facilities; others have practically none. If the facilities are inadequate, the branch manager has to improvise while he waits for management to respond to his request for whatever is most urgently needed. Here are some suggestions:

If there is no classroom, meetings can be held on the selling floor, in the branch restaurant, or in the employee cafeteria before store opening. Coffee and doughnuts constitute a nice gesture. By standing at the door to greet people as they arrive, the branch manager acknowledges the cooperation of those who come promptly, and offers a silent rebuke to the tardy ones.

If there are part-time and late shift people who cannot be reached through early sessions, the store restaurant can be used in late afternoon for a second meeting. For something really special, attendance at the morning meeting should be required; as an alternative, designate one person in each department to be responsible for passing along the content of the meeting to those who missed it.

In addition to large meetings, department managers should have brief "huddles" with their people frequently—some early in the day, some late. A five-minute cloakroom conference with the afternoon part-timers is better than no meeting at all. One successful New England merchant does the major part of his training through just such short, capsule meetings, one a day, in every department.

Another approach is for the branch manager to invite key resources to send their representatives to speak to salespeople in the appropriate departments. Usually, these men come frequently to the main store, but cannot spare the time to visit all the branches individually. So they tend to visit none. A definite invitation from the branch manager himself, however, changes the situation in the resource's eyes.

For such a project, the buyer concerned should be asked to nominate the resources to be contacted. He will know which ones are important in terms of their line's value to the store, and which ones can send representatives with real ability to inspire salespeople. If the buyer interests himself for the branch, all the better!

Films of all kinds—slide, motion, sound, silent—are increasingly available from many sources for training purposes. If the branch lacks a projector, and has no camera department from which to borrow one, the audio-visual material can nevertheless be used. Hobbyists on the store staff are usually happy to lend and operate their own equipment. Or the equipment may be rented, at modest fees, from camera specialty shops.

Exhibits, if there is no classroom in which to display them, can be set up in the employee cafeteria, or near the employee lockers, or wherever the necessary light, wall space, and employee traffic come together.

Using the Printed Word

In training salespeople, the printed word is not a particularly good substitute for personal contact, but it is an excellent supplement. One top training director always gives salespeople something in writing to take with them from a meeting—a summary of the points covered, some selling sentences for the merchandise shown, etc.

Another training director has a system that works admirably in branch stores with many short-shift employees. Near each cash register is a loose-leaf manual, with current regulations and other information all salespeople should know. When a change is made, the department manager is responsible for having everyone under his jurisdiction read and initial the new page. Then it is inserted in the book.

Similar procedure suggests itself for getting fashion information to the sales staff. Whether or not the fashion coordinator sends a fashion show to the branches, or invites branch people downtown to see such a showing, it is a good idea to have a booklet on the current fashion trends in each appropriate department. This could be an adaptation of the booklets that buying offices generally prepare each season for the store's merchandise managers. Then, as the season develops, pages can be added or changed as needed.

For some departments, a fairly high degree of expertise is required in selling—for example corsets, or shoes, which require fitting. A buyer with time to coach the staff adequately at each and every branch is rare. So is a department manager knowledgeable enough to tell the salespeople all they should know without help from the buyer. Yet no branch can afford to get the name for giving its customers unsatisfactory fit.

If a branch has a problem in such departments, self-teaching manuals can fill the gap, or most of it. NRMA has one on shoes, the "Retail Shoe Sales Training Manual," by Seymour Helfant. Trade publications and resources in other fields also produce self-teaching material. If a buyer knows that the branch wants these aids and will use them, he can usually track down something suitable.

Training Never Stops

Everyone needs stimulation on his job. Store heads go to conventions; branch managers attend seminars; buyers get to the market. All come back with fresh viewpoints and new zest for their jobs.

Salespeople continue, year after year, in the same store and often in the same section of the same department. Any renewal of zest for them has to come from executives in the store itself. Call it training; call it stimulation. If it isn't done, either on the training director's initiative or at the request of the branch manager, the selling staff grows stale, and productivity drops.

Contests and drives are parts of the training effort. So are seminars, especially for the more experienced salespeople, because these people have sat through any number of meetings over the years, and need something different to wake them up.

A successful seminar reported by one training director was on the theme of the salesperson's importance to the store. Top management and heads of the various store activities took turns as discussion leaders, always with the objective of showing salespeople how their work on the floor affected the success of management, merchandising, protection, or whatever the leader represented. Another successful seminar invited a dozen of the store's best salespeople to talk about their favorite selling techniques. A tape recording of the session provided material for training the store's less skilled salespeople.

Any of these projects can be initiated and carried through by a training department on its own, of course. But they are infinitely more effective if they are done with the active participation of the branch manager himself. Whether he suggests the device, or merely approves one planned by the training department, the branch manager who puts himself into the picture lets the salespeople know that their work (their productivity) is important to him.

Current Merchandise Information

One vital element in the training of salespeople can come only from the buyer himself—current information about the merchandise he has bought, his reasons for selecting it, points that make it acceptable to customers, availability of additional supply, etc. Among the devices with which stores have successfully expedited the flow of such information are these:

• The buyer dictates a memo to all branches about incoming new merchandise. Salespeople know what to look for when the goods arrive and what to say when speaking to customers.

• The buyer holds a meeting with main store salespeople. A tape is made of the talk, including questions and answers, to be played back at the branches.

• A conference phone hookup is made of all branches and the main store. Each buyer has a scheduled period for addressing salespeople. If specific items of merchandise are to be discussed, examples are sent to the branch or pulled from branch stocks beforehand, so that they can be exhibited on cue. Questions can be asked at any location and answered by the buyer.

• Fashion presentations are worked up at the main store early each season. Branch managers are called in to see the presentation early at the main store. Later, the show "goes on the road" to each branch in turn, with the fashion coordinator acting as commentator and distributing give-away leaflets to summarize trend information for salespeople. The store which uses this procedure applies it to women's wear, but it is easily adapted to men's, children's, or home goods divisions.

• Department managers are called into the parent store at intervals, to attend merchandise presentations to the salespeople, or presentations developed especially for them. They carry back the story to their own branch salespeople.

• The vice president in charge of branches schedules educational market trips for branch department managers, who accompany buyers into showrooms and bring information and enthusiasm back to their units.

• Buyers send to a central point any material of interest to branches—memos, clips from publications, material from promotion kits supplied by resources and publications, etc. A responsible individual arranges to photocopy and distribute the material from all buyers to all branches. Editing is sometimes done. Any buyer

NEWS ABOUT YOUR MERCHANDISE

Dept.____31_____   Date____April 25____

    We have just sent you a new personalized stationery album of

the Drew collection. This is the most colorful and distinctive collection

of writing papers.

    Notice that all the papers have lined envelopes and hand

bordered papers. Some have two color borders.

    These papers are all top quality paper for easier writing.

    Be sure to call your customers attention to this new collection

of writing paper. When they see these papers, I'm sure you will be

taking their orders.

Also, remember, the delivery on these papers is only three weeks.

                              Regards,

                              D. Jones

Merchandise Information--As simple a notation as this one,
jotted down or dictated by the buyer and duplicated for
transmission to all branches, alerts department managers
and salespeople to new, incoming merchandise and its
selling points. The less elaborate, the easier to use.

EXHIBIT 17

negligent in this respect is obviously so to the person in charge of the project as well as to all branch managers.

• Motion pictures and slide films are made at the main store. Volunteers model new fashions, and amateur equipment is operated by volunteer camera hobbyists. Since only film and processing are purchased, the cost of sending a filmed fashion show or other material to the branches is low. Small branches have shown these films in stockrooms when no other space was available.

• Television tape is being used experimentally for the same purpose, and in the same way.

The Game Is Worth the Candle

A dramatic example of what good selling alone can accomplish was provided in an experiment several years ago. A community selected one store as a guinea pig, and for a month, staffed that store with the best salespeople from the entire area. Merchandising, management, promotion, incentives, were unchanged. The only factor that could be responsible for improved sales was the selling staff itself. When the normal, average staff was replaced by a corps of crack salespeople, the increase in sales was more than 20 per cent.

Obviously, it pays the branch manager to interest himself in how his salespeople are selected and trained.

CHAPTER 15

SALES PRODUCTIVITY—II

Stepping up sales productivity involves an unremitting war on waste: scheduling and budgeting manpower on the selling floor, and avoiding every possible lost step or minute.

Budgeting Needs

Predicting the flow of customer traffic and the corresponding need for sales help is like predicting the weather: there are signs to study, conclusions to be drawn, and plenty of chances for error. Yet advance planning and budgeting of help must be done if costs are to be kept within bounds.

In theory, it should be possible to apply each department's past selling cost figure (sales salaries as a percentage of net sales) against its planned sales, and thus to come up with an estimate of how much it can afford to spend on sales help each day or week. From that figure, using the prevailing rates of pay, one can work back to the number of man-hours of help it can afford.

In actuality, nothing quite takes the place of observing conditions on the floor, taking register readings, making notes, and discussing the situation with the department manager. Dollar figures and percentages alone cannot take into account all the factors that need to be considered, such as physical area to be covered, price lines involved, planned promotions, changes in location or merchandise mix of department, and so on. That is one reason why some authorities prefer to budget sales help first in terms of the number of people expected to be needed by the day, department, or even hour, and then to work back to a dollar figure.

157

Checking Validity of Budget

There are several devices a branch manager can use to check on the accuracy with which the size of the selling staff meets his unit's needs. Understaffed as well as overstaffed conditions are both cause for concern, it should be remembered. A department that turns away customers for lack of help is every bit as costly to the store as one whose salespeople stand about idly.

Departmental "book." Compare the sales of each department (or group of departments, or classifications, as the case may be) with the selling salaries charged to it day by day.

Hourly chart. Take hourly register readings and chart the number of transactions in an area. Superimpose on this chart an hourly chart of the number of salespeople on the floor. Investigate those areas in which the two curves vary widely, after allowance is made for stock checks and other work that salespeople do in the slow hours.

Absence reports. Check any department that consistently gets along without extra help when some of its people are absent. It may be overstaffed, or its excessively economical manager may be losing sales by neglecting to ask for needed help. Also check into conditions in any department that has consistently higher absence rates than others. Unpleasant physical or emotional climate can cause high absences, and can interfere with productivity on the job, too.

Errors reports. Any area that has more than the prevailing rate of error may be understaffed, and its salespeople may be too hurried to maintain a good level of accuracy. Or it may be overstaffed, and its people may be doing poor work out of boredom.

Comparison with last year. Check the number of salespeople as compared with the previous year, and with the number budgeted for the current year. Investigate outstandingly large variations in actual or budgeted staff from year to year, particularly if there is no apparent relationship to variations in sales.

Turnover. Check into any department with higher turnover of help than the branch as a whole, in search of correctable causes. New employees are costly to hire and train and are seldom as productive as those who have been on the job for some time.

Shopping reports. Scan shopping reports for indications that any of the departments shopped are overstaffed or understaffed.

Overstaffed and Understaffed Areas

Even with the most careful of estimates, however, there are bound to be times when a department is temporarily overstaffed. Up to a certain point, the slack can be taken up within the department by stock work, clerical jobs, or notes and telephone calls to personal followings. Beyond that point, department managers should be trained to make some of their people available for reassignment to busier areas.

Depending upon store system and equipment, such reassignments may be made for a day, a week, or an hour. In either case, it is a good idea to let the salespeople know when they are hired that they may be asked to help out in other departments, and that such requests are a tribute to their ability to adapt quickly to new merchandise. If this is not done beforehand, a spur-of-the-moment transfer may cause resentment or uneasiness, and affect the quality of the selling adversely.

When a department is temporarily understaffed, it is seldom economical to hire and train a new employee for a brief period. Other possibilities are:

Contingent list. Departing employees who have given satisfactory performance should be asked by department managers and by the personnel office if they are interested in being recalled for future assignments. Since they already know the store and its system, and are familiar with the merchandise of one or more departments, they can be ready for productive work on the selling floor with only minimum preparation. A convenient way of maintaining such a list is on a card file, with each card tabbed to indicate the types of merchandise the person has sold.

EMERGENCY CREW LIST

Store _____

| Employee Name & Time Card No. | Departments in which worked or trained | | Date Last Worked |
	Sales Supporting (specify)	Selling Dept.:	
M. Jones No. 1297	Stock, Hosiery		6/30
B. Brown No. 3217		Cost. Jewelry	6/30
H. Taylor No. 3427		Hosiery	6/30
R. Smith No. 2286	Marker, gloves, scarfs		7/15

Emergency Crew List--A simple record like this one
keeps track of experienced employees who have given
satisfaction, are willing to return if called, and are
capable of performing productive work at short notice,
within minimum training. Each department manager.
or supervisor of non-selling activities can maintain
his own record; the personnel office can maintain more
elaborate records for the entire store, with names,
addresses, and telephones.

EXHIBIT 18

Flying squad. This is an elite group of salespeople, selected and
trained to fit into any department at a moment's notice. Members
of the squad are paid more than other salespeople, and are regarded as promotion material. Their higher hourly rate is more
than offset by their superior productivity. And they save the costs
involved in interviewing, hiring, and training new people for
brief assignments.

Work Schedules

The night openings that characterize suburban branch activity have led to the development of a variety of work schedules for salespeople, and have shed some light on how the hours of work affect the availability of desirable, productive workers.

The use of part-time help permits infinite variations in scheduling and makes selling jobs particularly attractive to housewives. Hours like 11:00 to 4:00, or 2:00 to 6:00, or 12:00 to 5:00, interfere little with their home responsibilities yet bring them into the store at its busiest periods.

Other variations, not necessarily aimed at housewives, include two full weekdays plus half or all of Saturday; four half-days plus one full day; two or three evenings plus Saturday. A good deal depends upon the pattern of customer traffic, the sort of people who are locally available, the maximum number of hours a part-timer can work each week without adding to the branch's fringe benefits bill.

According to many branch managers, housewives who are attracted to part-time selling are usually women who enjoy meeting the public and who take their responsibilities seriously. They are among the most dependable and conscientious of salespeople. They are generally not promotion material, however, because they avoid any career aspirations that could interfere with their home responsibilities.

"Moonlighters" who work evening shifts and Saturdays, in addition to a full week's work elsewhere, are reported to be of an even higher type. Some are housewives, who can work only when the husbands are home to sit with the children. Others are teachers or business people, temporarily supplementing their normal earnings. Turnover is likely to be high among them, however, as compared to daytime workers.

The Two-Platoon System

The two-platoon system combines full-time, "moonlight" and part-time workers. It calls for a crew of salespeople and super-

SCHEDULE OF PLANNED HOURS

Store _Westwood_   Dept. No. _32_   Week Ending _12/9/67_

Employee Name	Time Card No.	Mon.	Tues.	Wed.	Thurs.	Fri.	Sat.	Tot. Hours
M. Jones	142	9/6	1/10	9/6	✗	9/6	9/6	40
R. Smith	168	1/10	✗	6/10	6/10	6/10	✗	20
B. Green	210	✗	9/6	1/10	9/6	9/6	9/6	40
M. Black	215	✗	✗	✗	6/10	6/10	9/6	16
S. Jennings	412	9/6	9/6	9/6	9/6	✗	9/6	40
H. Johnson	315	6/10	6/10	✗	✗	✗	9/6	16

Coverage	AM	MID	PM	EVE	AM	MID	PM	EVE	AM	MID	PM	EVE	AM	MID	PM	EVE	AM	MID	PM	EVE	AM	MID	PM	EVE	Tot. Hrs.
Assigned	2	3	3	2	2	3	3	2	2	3	3	2	2	2	2	2	2	2	2	2	2	5	5	5 –	172
Budgeted	2	3	2	3	2	3	2	3	2	3	2	3	2	3	2	3	1	2	3	2	5	5	5	–	175

Dept. Manager _J. Wilson_

A simple form assists in managing assignment of time. In this example, the department uses a combination of part and full time employees, six in all, to provide never less than two on the floor at any given time during the week, and with almost everyone on duty Saturday. Actual and planned coverage are totaled at bottom by time of day: (A.M. = 9a.m. to 12 noon; MID= 12 noon to 3 p.m.; P.M. = 3 p.m. to 6 p.m.; EVE= 6 p.m. to 9 p.m.)

EXHIBIT 19

visors to work five full days, Monday through Friday, with no night or Saturday hours. Free weekends and free evenings, say the stores on this system, attract a very high type of help. A second platoon of salespeople and supervisors works evenings and Saturdays. Part-timers supplement both crews as needed.

Usually, the late shift concentrates on selling. Stock work and displays and departmental rearrangements are carried out by the day crew in the slow morning hours. To provide liaison between the two groups, some stores maintain a log in each section, which is turned over to the night supervisor by his opposite number on the day staff. Another device is to allow a 15-minute overlap in the hours of work. This puts both shifts on duty together long enough so that word can be passed along informally about any special problems or conditions.

The two-platoon system is not for every branch, however, and particularly not for those that get their main customer traffic during evenings and Saturdays. In one such branch, the personnel manager tries to have a core of the best trained, most experienced full-time people on hand at such times. Her schedule for full-time help: Five full days a week, including Saturday, and with one workday each week that begins after lunch and continues until closing time.

The War on Waste

Many a retailer who is horrified at the waste involved in a needless markdown fails to realize that there is a lot of needless waste in the way salespeople use their time. Much of it is management's fault, not theirs.

Salespeople are not likely to bring time wasters to management's attention. Unless the branch manager or his aides observe and correct the conditions, the selling staff will probably plod along, accepting unnecessary difficulties as part of the job, and assuming that, if the store pays for their time, it has the privilege of wasting it.

Here are some quite common, and usually quite avoidable, wasters of salespeople's time:

Distant registers. If the salesperson has to walk across the floor to a distant register each time she rings up a sale, the service in her department will be badly slowed down just when it most needs to be lively—when customer traffic is heavy. Some customers will lose patience and walk out. Others will mark the store down in their books as slow and pokey, and go elsewhere in future. Shoplifters will see a glorious opportunity opening before them each time a girl starts her trek to the register.

Wrapping desks. Poorly located, they create the same problem as distant registers. Poorly equipped or poorly stocked, they slow service down. Someone on each floor, or in each section of the floor, should have the responsibility for checking supplies at each wrapping desk every morning and, at busy times, at intervals during the day. A wheeler with bags and rolls of paper of various sizes can make the rounds and stock several wrapping stations on a single trip. A salesperson is likely to go off the floor on a hunt for bags of one needed size and then, an hour later, go off again for another size.

Gift wrap. If any gift wrapping is done by salespeople, supplies of tissue, boxes, and elasticized ribbon should be readily available, to make the process quicker and easier. During peak gift shopping periods supplies of these items should be checked and replenished at specified intervals during the day.

Marking. Spot checks on signs and price tickets should be a continuing assignment for the branch manager or an aide. If the marking is unclear, or if the signs have fallen off bins of non-marked goods, the salesperson loses time while she seeks to ascertain the price or size of an item—and may sell it at the wrong price.

Cumbersome system. If store system for handling transactions of certain types involves the salespeople in unduly laborious record-keeping or telephoning, an effort should be made to change procedures by calling the attention of appropriate main store executives to the condition.

Hard-to-use supplies. Supplies that are hard to use slow down sales productivity by lengthening the time required to complete a transaction and by wearing out the salespeople and decreasing their effectiveness early in the day. Among the villains: rolls of paper too heavy for easy handling, boxes that open like puzzles, paper cutters that perform poorly, supplies that are stored on high or very low shelves, gummed-paper dispensers that hold less than a day's supply of paper and water, cord so light that it has to be wound several times around a box for safety, pens that require coaxing, hangers that let garments slip off too easily.

Check writers. In busy periods, assign a clerk, possibly from the office staff, to write sales checks and complete transactions for salespeople, so that they can continue to circulate and handle customers uninterruptedly.

Register tapes. The thrifty practice of using a roll of register tape down to the last inch before replacing it can cost more than it is worth in selling time. Tapes that are, say, three-quarters used, should be replaced at store opening, to avoid the loss of wasteful selling time (and selling opportunity) if the tape runs out in a busy period.

Stock arrangement. Within the limits of what good merchandise presentation requires, stock should be arranged with an eye to saving steps for salespeople. Distant reserves and inadequate space for floor stock can add up to a lot of selling time lost in going or sending for what the customer wants. If selling space is cramped and the stock on the floor must be kept light, then fill-ins should be scheduled every morning and at specified intervals during the day.

Fitting rooms. If salespeople have long trek to fitting rooms and lose too much time from the floor standing by during try-ons, consider a "hostess" to be on duty as a general aide to all customers in fitting rooms during rush periods.

Merchandise. One of the saddest of time wasters in selling can be the merchandise itself. If the branch is out of a staple, or if its assortment is weak where demand is strong, the most efficient and capable salespeople cannot sell as much as they should. They lose sales, lose customers, lose heart. Vigilance in merchandising is part of the effort to step up sales productivity.

Motivation

Nothing quite increases sales productivity like the salesperson's own desire to produce. Those who are really eager to do a good job will be quick to fill their idle time productively, and to do the best they can with every selling opportunity that confronts them.

Planning and paper work can do much to keep costs down and selling productivity up, but good motivation can do even more. The suggestions contained in the chapters of this book on leadership, communication, and employee relations have special significance in this connection. A branch manager who can convey some of the substance of these chapters to his various department managers can look forward to more intelligent help from them in increasing sales productivity.

CHAPTER 16

SALES PRODUCTIVITY AND EMPLOYEE RELATIONS

Productivity on any job is closely related to the degree of satisfaction the employee feels with his work, with the firm that employs him, and with the supervisor from whom he takes orders. Among branch salespeople, good employee relations are sufficiently important to deserve special attention from the manager, over and above his efforts to demonstrate leadership and inspire good morale in the store as a whole.

The salespeople merit this special attention because:

- they are the largest single group of employees in the branch,
- they are the productive group, since they perform the branch's major function, selling,
- they are in direct contact with the branch's customers and cannot help conveying something of their attitude to them,
- many of them are in social contact with branch customers and can brighten or dim the store's image among these people.

The salespeople, in short, can do a great deal to make or break the branch's position in the community—and the branch manager's future in the store organization. However capable and dedicated his store's personnel staff may be in the matter of maintaining good employee relations, the forward-looking branch manager accepts the maintenance of troop morale as a major responsibility of his own.

This chapter is by way of being a check list of things a branch manager can do, without necessarily waiting for direction from the main store, in order to maintain good relationships with (and top productivity from) salespeople and other employees at his unit.

New Employees

Keep a watchful eye on interviewing and hiring procedures to make sure new employees are not mishandled, oversold, or otherwise started off on the wrong foot.

Require a list of new employees from the employment office at specified intervals. Make a point of greeting each one by name as a welcome new member of the team.

Prepare or ask the personnel executive to prepare an induction check list of all the points to be covered by sponsors and department managers when a new sales person reports for duty: locations of merchandise, supplies, registers; facilities for eating and resting; safety rules; names of other people in department; other needed information. In large branches, require a sheet to be made out and returned to Personnel for each new employee. In smaller branches, supply the check list simply as a reminder to those responsible for inducting the new employee.

Ask questions of new people to see if the required information, as above, has been supplied and understood. This should not be a catechism, but a friendly inquiry like, "Has anyone showed you around the store?" or "Have you been told about the discount you get on your own purchases?" or "Have you been to our lunch room yet? How do you like it?"

Make sure new employees know about benefits to which they are entitled and to which they will become entitled after a period of time—tenure, health insurance, discounts, etc. If there is no booklet for employees on the subject, urge the personnel staff to prepare one.

Impress upon department managers that the salespeople working under them are important to them and to the store. Urge them to keep a friendly, watchful eye on new employees.

Check personally and ask department managers to check also on the way in which sponsors perform their function. A bossy,

For_____ (Name of Supervisor or Sponsor) _____

INDUCTION CHECK LIST FOR SPONSORS AND SUPERVISORS

Please check off each item after you have discussed it
with the new employee and are sure it is understood.
Return finished form to_____

New Employee's Name_____

Position_____ Dept._____ Starting Date_____

Check as covered	Information to Be Given New Employee
_____	Job description, duties
_____	Pay days, pay station
_____	Time card, rack, mispunches
_____	Hours, including relief, lunch, dinner
_____	Overtime, lateness, absenteeism
_____	Location of merchandise and stock rooms
_____	Salesbooks, registers, other forms
_____	Where to obtain supplies
_____	Safety rules
_____	Reporting of unsafe conditions
_____	Accident reports
_____	Eating facilities
_____	Rest room, lockers, parking
_____	Dress Regulations
_____	Introduction to co-workers in department
_____	Employee shopping
_____	

Supervisor's or sponsor's initials_____ Date_____

- Induction Check List--A check list of this kind, with whatever items
are appropriate to the activity and the store, serves several purposes.
It reminds the sponsor or supervisor of the points to cover with each
new employee. It shows the new employee the importance management
attaches to giving him a good start in his new job. By requiring signature
and return, it emphasizes to the sponsor or supervisor that perfunctory
induction of new employees is not sufficient.

EXHIBIT 20

irritable sponsor can play havoc with morale. A friendly, patient person, who perhaps goes to lunch with a new salesperson on the first day, is a more desirable choice.

Employee Facilities

Personally, or through an aide, make unannounced inspection visits to all employee facilities to make sure they are clean, comfortable, and in good condition—lounge, washrooms, cafeteria, locker rooms, parking area. Make sure light in rest and locker areas is adequate; low wattage bulbs make for dingy, depressing effect. Especially is this so for salespeople fresh from a bright selling floor.

If there is an employee cafeteria, examine the possibility of running it on a no-profit basis, to provide low-cost meals. Insist upon at least one nutritious but inexpensive special on each day's menu.

Install vending machines exclusively for employee use to dispense coffee, soft drinks, cigarettes. Examine possibility of cut-price, non-profit operation. Check performance of machines regularly.

Obtain television set for employee lounge or cafeteria. If there is no budget for a set, it may be possible to get the loan of a demonstration model from the branch's TV department or from a nearby television and appliance store. The lender may reasonably expect sales to result from this courtesy.

Set up an employee bulletin board for the exclusive use of employees themselves. A volunteer can take charge of it. Suggest that it be used for "swap" offers, announcements of rooms and apartments wanted or for rent, pets wanted or offered, club meetings, bowling leagues, lessons wanted or offered—anything to do with the personal interests of the employees, rather than business.

"Happy Family" Touches

Have a branch house organ, even if it is no more than a single mimeographed sheet, in addition to the column or page devoted to the branch in the store's own magazine.

Send a birthday greeting, hand signed by the branch manager, to each employee each year. Employment records show birth dates.

On the usual gift occasions—weddings, babies, illness—send a personal gift and greeting from the branch manager.

Send a personal Christmas card to each employee's home in the branch manager's name.

After major sales, send a thank-you letter in branch manager's name to home of each employee who participated.

Maintain a manager's bulletin board for messages from the branch manager to the staff. Include messages of commendation, as well as announcements and rules.

If the store offers scholarships to employees' gifted children, maintains a blood bank for employees' families, or provides other less than commonplace benefits, publicize these at frequent intervals—house organ, bulletin board, mention at meetings, etc., plus announcement of any recipients.

Recognize employee anniversaries with a greeting, a rose, or other small token, after one year of service, five, ten, etc.

If branch is not too large, storewide dinners, theater parties, and picnics are good for morale. In large branches, encourage department managers to arrange get-togethers of this kind for their own groups. The branch does not have to pick up the check on all such events; some can be Dutch-treat, with a slight subsidy from the branch.

Send personal notes of commendation to individual salespeople who merit it—those with top shopping reports, those praised by customers, those with superior sales and error records, etc. Post copies on manager's and employees' bulletin boards, to invite congratulation by co-workers.

In Sickness and in Health

Organize sympathy-and-congratulation committee, to send gifts, flowers, condolences, as occasion warrants, to employees who are ill, bereaved, engaged, parents of new babies, etc.

Organize sick visits. If branch has no visiting nurse, require each department manager to arrange visits from the department to any salesperson who is absent because of extended illness.

Check with store nurse or personnel office on departments with high records of sickness and absenteeism. A tense, irascible supervisor may be the cause of a health problem. Or there may be problems of heating or ventilation that should be corrected. Physical or psychological, conditions which produce health hazards also detract from sales productivity.

Request health and safety leaflets from the insurance companies that provide the store's health, life, and liability coverage. Distribute to all employees. Post on bulletin boards. Keep extras on file in nurse's or personnel office for employees who may later have personal or family problems in fields covered.

Assign store nurse, personnel executive, or other aide to keep abreast of community health programs and facilities. Post appropriate notices on bulletin board.

Designate an executive to keep informed of sources of subsidized help for employees or their families when there is an expensive illness—foundations, public assistance, clinics, etc., as well as any benefits available from store itself. Post name of this executive permanently on employee bulletin board, in locker area, and similar places.

Whether or not store has program of periodic health examinations, encourage employees to accept free check-ups for diabetes, tuberculosis, etc., whenever these are offered in area.

If local blood bank permits, organize branch blood bank, so that employee contributions are credited to "fund" on which all may draw.

If preventive inoculations are available against flu and other contagious diseases, set personal example by accepting. Urge all to follow.

Rewards and Incentives

One branch has a turkey raffle at Thanksgiving. Winners get everything needed for the dinner. *But* drawing is open only to superior salespeople. Superiority is based on sales, attendance, seniority, courtesy, commendations, or whatever elements branch manager most wants to stress.

The branch manager himself can host a buffet at the store after periods of special strain, like Christmas, major sales, inventory-taking.

Department managers can host similar buffets or dinners after major departmental efforts.

Mystery shoppers, paid or volunteer, can present tokens, cards, dollar bills, etc., to salespeople who are especially helpful. One branch with a consumer advisory board gives each member of the board a card, to be handed at some time during her year of service to an outstanding salesperson. The salesperson gets a small award and a lot of very public commendation. Another branch sends a letter in the manager's name once or twice a year to each charge customer; the customer presents the letter to a courteous salesperson. Salesperson gets small cash award and an entry on her record.

Follow promotion-from-within program as far as possible. Publicize promotions throughout branch. If any branch employee has transferred to a bigger job at the main store or another branch and has had subsequent promotions, report these, too.

Invite salespeople with outstanding records (sales, attendance, error-free work, etc.) to an annual manager's dinner or similar celebration.

Remind department managers at frequent intervals that outstanding performance of any kind should be acknowledged—as should outstandingly poor work. Offer to write or speak to top performers who have earned congratulations, and to help with those who present problems.

Teaching Management

Keep an open door for department managers who believe they are not getting the best possible work from their salespeople. They may need help—or they may simply need reassurance.

Urge department managers to explain the aims and objectives

of their departments to salespeople. Knowledge breeds interest, and interest breeds enthusiasm.

Teach the technique of getting better performance:

- Praise in public.
- Correct in private.
- Never assume that an error was made deliberately.
- Correct constructively. Instead of scolding for poor performance, say, "Next time, do it this way ...." and give reasons why that is the better way.
- Never allow outstandingly good or poor performance to go unnoticed.

Insist upon courtesy to and from subordinates. Watch especially any young, ambitious junior executives who seem to patronize older salespeople. Remind them that, without the willing help of these very salespeople, their departments and their careers can collapse.

Turnabout

Occasional reversals of roles within the store are fun, and improve employee relations. Sales, too, sometimes. When employees can be customers and executives can serve as salespeople, a good deal of friendly spirit is generated.

Open house is a familiar version of this idea. It may be held just before a branch opens, or at the start of the Christmas season. The store is not open to the public, but for an evening or for a few hours on a Sunday, it is open to employees and their families. Executives man the registers and write up the sales checks.

Salespeople enjoy the special service and the chance to show off to their relatives. At the same time, their shopping tours refresh them on the locations of departments and the nature of the merchandise offered in areas other than their own.

Employees-only clearances are a less common version, held on similar pattern by some high fashion stores, whose merchandise is normally priced out of reach of the average salesperson's income. A special evening is set aside for the sale, and merchandise at drastic markdowns is brought from all over the store to a designated spot, such as the employee lunchroom. Executives sell; salespeople buy.

Skits intended to dramatize good and poor selling techniques seem to make a particular hit with salespeople when executives act the part of the slothful or stupid clerks.

Ratings, Reviews, Promotions

Before semi-annual ratings and reviews are made, call together all department managers and others who will be required to pass judgment on subordinates. Explain purpose of reviews and basis of ratings. Invite discussion. Warn against perfunctory reviews.

Spot-check review reports to see that they are being thoughtfully done.

In addition to whatever the personnel staff does, arrange to speak personally to the best-rated employees. Also, to interview any employee whose formerly fine record now shows a poor report. Also, to check up on some with very poor records to see if there is any correctable fault in the working conditions, supervision, method of hiring, etc.

Use promotions as a means of getting excellent performance from salespeople. The promotions, however, should be in line with the personal goals of the individuals, if they are to accomplish anything substantial. To a saleswoman with no executive aspirations, a desirable promotion may be a transfer to a department where the selling is more challenging and the salary potential is larger than in her present spot. An ambitious girl, on the other hand, may consider no promotion worthy of that name unless it is to a job involving more responsibility than selling alone.

Preventive Maintenance

Preventive maintenance can be used in employee morale as well as in the care of buildings and equipment. Before sales productivity slips badly, signs of trouble may show themselves and invite investigation by the branch manager. Among them are:

- high absence records,
- high lateness records,
- high error reports,
- excessive shrinkage,
- high employee turnover,
- abnormal number of headaches and minor illnesses reported to store nurse,
  - general air of tenseness or sullenness in department,
  - high accident rate,
  - sloppy appearances of department or salespeople,
  - unenthusiastic participation in storewide contests.

Exit interviews provide an important index to conditions among the employees. The branch personnel staff probably has instructions from the main store as to how to conduct such interviews and what records to keep of them. If this is not the case, the branch manager should institute the procedure. The personnel director at the downtown store can help immeasurably in setting up the method and pointing out ways in which to analyze the information obtained.

Simple example: A basic question in exit interviews, particularly with employees who have done satisfactory work, is whether or not they would care to return in future to work at the store. Any department with a larger percentage of negative, evasive, or resentful replies than the rest should be investigated.

A branch manager, burdened with many other responsibilities, and in a store staffed with trained personnel workers, may wonder at times why he should also concern himself with the day to day problems of maintaining morale among employees in general and among salespeople in particular. The answer is clear. The store's good name and the manager's whole future are in their hands. Upon their productivity and attitude hinges his success.

CHAPTER 17

BRANCH PROFITS AND
MERCHANDISE HANDLING

Branch managers often fail to recognize the importance to profit of keeping a watchful eye on merchandise handling in their units —that is, on traffic, receiving, and marking, and the movement of goods within the store.

In this respect, they are not unique. Top management itself, in industry as well as in retailing, is also reported to be less than alert to the opportunities for improvement in this area. Yet the money involved is substantial and the profit leaks can be numerous indeed. Moreover, the rewards of developing a good, expense-conscious job usually include greater efficiency of operation and increased speed in getting goods to the selling floor.

Extent of Opportunity

Sheer unawareness of costs is often cited by experts as the reason for management's indifference to the savings to be culled in this area. Another reason frequently given is fragmented responsibility—the fact that no one person controls all the various elements that make up the cost of merchandise handling. Bits and pieces of the responsibility run through almost every part of the organization.

Branch managers, if they have a blind spot with respect to costs and wastes in merchandise handling, have an excuse for the oversight. The prevailing practice among branch-owning stores is to use central facilities for receiving, marking, and reserve stock. Since the work is not done under the branch manager's eye, he does not always realize that he should concern himself with it.

The simple fact is that no manager of traffic, receiving and marking, at the main store or in a branch, can effectively control all the loose ends of the merchandise handling operation. There are too many fingers in that particular pie. Everyone, from stock boy to merchandise manager, has a part to play if costs are to be kept down and performance is to be kept high. The responsibility is really storewide.

The Problem

The costs of merchandise handling are not readily separated from other expenses of the store. Some of the main elements, however, are highlighted in the FOR. (This is the *Financial and Operating Results of Department Stores,* published each year by the Controllers' Congress, NRMA.)

Recent figures show that inward transportation for department stores typically costs in the neighborhood of one and one-third percent of purchases. Material handling costs, as shown in the FOR for a normal year, were 1.36 percent of sales. Under this heading, the report includes receiving and marking, shuttle service, and maintenance of reserve stock.

There are no figures, however, to show the costs that really hurt: the markdowns, lost sales, and other merchandising casualties that arise when goods are unnecessarily slow in their journey from the vendor's shipping room to the branch's selling floor.

The elements of the problem are many and varied, and a surprising number of them are within the scope of the branch manager's job. Among these elements are: the frequency and size of orders placed; the area and facilities for receiving and marking; the paper work; the people assigned to the various tasks; the procedures; the possibilities in mechanization, EDP, and vendor marking.

Points to Check

Following this section, the balance of this chapter is virtually a check-list of points with which a branch manager should familiarize himself. These are areas into which to look in efforts to secure a better merchandise handling operation.

If procedures at the branch or involving the branch's contacts with the main store seem to need correction on any of these points, or if problems arise that seem to need the advice of an expert, the branch manager should call upon the main store's experts. As specialists in their own fields, a store's traffic manager, receiving manager and marking room head know sources, procedures, costs, equipment, and possible hazards. But, in their downtown headquarters, they may not be aware immediately that a problem exists at the branch. Alertness in bringing an actual or potential problem to their attention will put their collaboration at the branch's disposal before the situation becomes acute.

Placing Orders

If orders are placed directly by the branch, as is often the case with fill-ins of basic items, someone should be assigned to check every order for specific shipping instructions. Terms like "as before," "cheapest way," etc., should never be used.

Even for much-used resources, it is advisable to check occasionally with the buyer or the traffic department to be sure that the branch has up-to-date information on (1) preferred shipping instructions and (2) preferred minimum quantities.

Small orders should be avoided as much as possible. Most carriers have minimum rates, and it often happens that several small shipments cost much more for transportation than a single large shipment, many times their combined size, coming from the same point.

Small orders coming from a major center like New York are often shipped through a consolidator employed by the store, and thus present less of a cost problem than otherwise. To keep those that originate in other shipping points to a minimum, the branch manager should institute spot checks of re-order quantities on basic stocks, to make sure they are working out economically. He should instruct department managers to avoid unnecessary special orders; he should also encourage sales and stock people to report lows, instead of waiting for outs and the urgent need for special fill-ins.

It pays to know the point of origin for every shipment that is ordered. The manufacturer's mailing address is not always his shipping point; he may have an out-of-town plant or warehouse.

The f. o. b. terms to which the branch is entitled should be carefully checked. These can make a difference in the branch's costs. If the buyer has secured "f.o.b store," for example, that means the vendor pays all transportation charges. If he has obtained "f.o.b. carrier terminal," that means the vendor, rather than the store, pays for cartage from plant to rail, truck, or air terminal. Failure to mark such terms on the order may result in a shipment slipping through with all transportation costs charged to the branch.

If an order is placed for a large quantity, or for several items that should be sent in one shipment, it is wise to mark "One complete shipment" on the order. Otherwise, the vendor may split the shipment, and thus subject the branch to higher transportation charges.

In any special situation, the branch should check with the traffic manager, or ask the buyer to do so. If extra speed is needed, or there is reason to expect difficulties along the route, or to question the shipping instructions on the branch records, a check is advisable before passing the order through.

If the branch manager has not the time to make all these checks personally, he should instruct an assistant or secretary to take over this work, and make spot checks personally on the checker.

When Receiving Goods

Department managers should be trained to make sure each package has come by the route and with the f.o.b. terms that were specified on the order. If not, the traffic manager should be asked about charging back for any extra costs involved.

The same should be done with partial shipments, unless the vendor prepays the late shipments. Even so, it pays to let the buyer and traffic manager know. Perhaps the other branches, too, have been getting partial shipments from the same vendor, and there may be reason for the buyer to look into the situation.

The receiving staff should be instructed to set aside "problem" packages, such as those that are not covered by an order in the file. The branch manager or a designated assistant should be notified at once of such packages, so that someone with the authority to investigate and obtain clearance will get on the job promptly. To facilitate compliance with this rule, the name and telephone extension number of the persons to be called should be posted.

To clear such shipments promptly is important. Occasionally, the fault lies with an order-checking system that is susceptible to repeated bottlenecks. In such cases, the branch manager may have to institute changes of procedure. In any circumstances, however, he should be thoroughly familiar with the order-checking routine of his store, so that he or an aide can swing promptly into action when delays occur. Knowing whom to contact is often the sword that cuts the Gordian knots on "problem" shipments.

Immediate report should be required also of any packages that come damaged, and may involve claims against shipper or carrier. If the store prefers to have all such claims handled through the traffic manager's office at the main store, his name and telephone should be posted, along with instructions, in the receiving area.

If large incoming shipments are expected, as they would be just before a sale, the receiving manager should know well in advance, so that he can prepare the space and staff he will need. Department managers need to be reminded periodically about this.

At intervals, the receiving dock should be inspected to make sure that it has enough truck positions and enough space for efficient handling of the goods that arrive. If there is reason to believe that branch needs are outgrowing present facilities, that condition should be reported to the main store without delay. Until such time as branch receiving facilities can be expanded, emergency provisions can probably be made such as shunting at least part of the overload to the main store.

Reports to Require

To keep abreast of the receiving and marking situation, the branch manager should require from this department, weekly or more often, an aging report—a listing of all shipments remaining in the marking room after a specified standard—24 hours, 48 hours, or whatever the case may be. The report should show: receiving number; date of receipt; resource; number of units; department; reason for delay.

He should also require a daily carryover report—a simple running report of the amount of work carried over, whatever the reason. This differs from the aging report in that it simply shows the amount of work unfinished, whether an hour old or a week old, at the end of the day.

Finally, he should require a production report, weekly, showing the total productivity in units processed per working hour. This should be compared with figures for the same week of the preceding year and for each of several preceding weeks of the current year.

If orders are checked at the branch, similar reports should be required on that activity: aging report, carryover, and productivity.

When Receiving Transfers

Store routine for checking in transfers of merchandise must be followed to the letter: verifying the number of containers, checking their seals, etc. If the driver is required to present a trip sheet, it should be inspected and clocked as required.

Frequent small shipments, even when they originate in the main store rather than in the market, are more expensive to handle than fewer large deliveries. If any department seems to require abnormally frequent fill-ins, this situation would invite a check on

TWO-DAY OLD REPORT

Date ___9/9/67___

From ___I. M. ABEL___   To ___I. KAIRE___
Receiving Department Head   Branch Manager

The following merchandise has been received but at the close of this day has not been delivered to the selling floors. It will be two days old or more tommorrow morning.

Vendor Name and Number	Date Received	No. of Units	Description of Mdse.	Reason for Delay
Dresses Unlimited 693	9/6	1 carton	Jr. Dresses	Pkg. damaged
Glamour Blouses 562	9/8	36 pc	Miss Blouses	No order
Action Sportswear 828	9/8	54 pc	Miss Skirts	Sizes not as ordered. Buyrot.
Tomboy Shoes 436	9/4	48 pr	Boy's Shoes	ret to vendor
Sturdy Knit 828	9/7	36 pc	Miss Sweaters	no order buyer out of town

Aging Report--To keep merchandise from piling up in the receiving room, branch managers can require their receiving heads to make out reports of this kind at regular intervals, such as on two specified days of the week. Compilation of the report is in itself a reminder to the receiving head that he should keep after negligent buyers; appearance of an item on two successive lists is a reminder to the branch manager to bring his weight to bear on the problem. A similar report can be required on two other days of the week on pending returns-to-vendor.

EXHIBIT 21

CARRYOVER REPORT

	Previous carryover	Incoming	Production	Carryover (new)
Department _____ Week of _____				
M				
T				
W				
Th				
F				
S				

This simple report tells the managers at a glance the condition of his operating areas. If the previous carryover figure is matched by production, the manager can feel confident that the receiving and marking, wrapping and packing, etc. area reporting is generally maintaining a one day standard. A dangerous backlog build-up will become evident early enough to take corrective action. This is not a substitute for an aging report, since the carryover might seem in order quantitively, but could be old and getting older.

NOTE: The Monday afternoon's new carryover becomes the Tuesday morning's previous carryover.

EXHIBIT 22

the stock, model stock plan, stockroom space, and basic stock re-order quantities. Adjustment may be necessary.

If the time-lag between the request for merchandise and receipt at the branch is too great for the distance involved, it is a good plan to check with the main store. The delay may have been avoidable and perhaps can be prevented next time.

Night deliveries are sometimes used to bring transfers to branches at times when road travel is quicker and there is little or no congestion at the receiving dock. If factors at the branch make this procedure especially desirable or especially difficult, the main store should be informed. These factors are not always obvious to those who are not right on the spot and they may not exist at other branches.

When Marking Incoming Merchandise

It pays to make sure that working conditions are what they should be: clean, light, well ventilated rooms; supervisors who can take the stress of the job without making life difficult for subordinates; as steady a flow of work as can be managed.

Adjusting the staff to the size of the work load is important but not always easily done. In some situations, it may be possible to organize a flying squad of markers who are trained to handle merchandise of many kinds, and who can augment whatever specialized marking crews most need help. In other situations, a night crew, to work during evening store hours, after the day crews leave, may be a solution. Still another possibility is to maintain a list of markers who will come in on call, for a few days or a few weeks, as needed. If the marking room head has not tried such approaches, the branch manager may have to make the suggestion.

Vacations in the marking room should not be permitted during peak receiving months, such as late July and early August. On the other hand, they can generally be encouraged at peak selling times, like December, when receipts slack off.

At any time of year, however, every effort should be made to let the marking room know in advance that shipments are expected to arrive in larger quantities, or are tapering off, so that the person in charge can augment or reduce his staff accordingly. It should not be taken for granted that the marking chief will anticipate peaks and valleys on his own, or that department managers will continue to notify him if they are not reminded periodically of the need to do so.

The flow of merchandise through the marking area should be planned so that there is a minimum of lifting and carrying, minimum back-tracking, and minimum rehandling of opened merchandise between the marking room and the sales floor. A good principle is to bring the merchandise and supplies to the personnel as far as possible, rather than require unnecessary moving about on the part of the markers.

Carrying a small backlog of work over at the end of each day is a good idea. It makes sure that markers have something on which to begin when they report in the morning, while waiting for new deliveries to come through.

A "hold" area is needed for problem merchandise—for example, when the retail prices have not been indicated by the buyer. The name and telephone extension of a designated person should be posted, so that the markers will know whom to notify for follow-through with the buyer concerned.

The receiving manager at the main store should be invited to visit the branch department at intervals. He is up to date on new equipment, new methods, and new procedures, and may be able to suggest improvements.

The marking equipment in the branch should be checked periodically against the size and nature of the work-load. To be over-equipped is sometimes quite as expensive as to be under-equipped. If some machines seem to be idle most of the time, perhaps the marking manager at the main store or another branch can take them and put them to use.

The flow of paper work should be studied. If the system doesn't fit the branch, or if it isn't adequately understood by the people working with it, there may be unnecessary delays. And delays in getting merchandise to the selling floor are costly.

Moving Merchandise

Wherever possible, paper should move rather than merchandise. If bulky items can be ordered out of the warehouse or main store for delivery directly to the customer's home, that is often cheaper than loading up the branch with a large supply.

Opportunities for mechanization should not be ignored. The branch may not have needed much by way of fork-lifts, conveyors, etc. when it first opened, but with the passage of time its activities may have reached the point where such equipment would pay off.

The physical demands imposed by handling the merchandise, even within selling departments, should be considered. If women employees are selling heavy or bulky merchandise, then male stock help, even part time, may be a time and money saver.

People and Productivity

Selection of supervisors for receiving, marking and stock work should be done with great care. The ability to create a team is important, and so is an open mind about new ways of handling the work.

Up to a certain point, an otherwise well qualified supervisor can take over, and acquire the needed technical background from working with the experts at the main store. And up to a certain point, a person new to supervisory duties, but familiar with receiving, marking, and stock work, can be coached in how to classify and describe jobs, hire, train, and supervise people.

If electronic data processing is used to control stocks and sales, it is important that everyone understands the steps for which he is responsible. The EDP reports can be no more accurate than the data the receivers and markers feed into the machine on receipts, returns, and transfers.

Progress can be checked regularly by comparing costs and production figures from season to season and year to year. A look behind the figures, too, may reveal outside elements that contribute to improvement or the absence thereof. Changes in carrier rates, new methods of vendor packing, the spread of vendor preticketing—these are among the cost factors that do not remain static.

A show of interest on the part of the branch manager is most desirable. Nothing spurs the laggard or encourages the timid to put forth suggestions quite as effectively as a friendly visit from the head of the house.

Prepare for the Future

Occasionally, on a trip to the main store, the branch manager should invest the time for a visit with the head of traffic, receiving, and marking there. An hour of seeing what he is doing, and why, is a good help toward preparing to cope with situations that may develop in the branch—or in some future assignment to a larger branch.

The trend among branch-owning stores is to make their new units larger and further away and more self-sufficient than those they have now. Thus, although prevailing practice is to concentrate receiving and marking operations as much as possible at the main store, this may not always be the case.

Among branch managers who participated in the surveys that guided this book, 37 per cent already handle most of their own receiving and marking under their own roofs. Receiving and marking is also an area in which many contributing branch heads said they would like greater authority in future.

Time and study invested in merchandise handling operations can pay immediate dividends in efficiency and expense reduction while laying the groundwork for helping the branch manager meet larger future responsibilities in this area.

CHAPTER 18

KEEPING EXPENSES DOWN

Expenses are like weeds. Ignore them for what seems only the wink of an eye, and they grow out of all reason. Blitzkriegs against them produce only temporary benefits. Steady, unremitting effort keeps them within bounds.

At the branch, the manager is the logical person to spearhead the necessary continuing campaign against unnecessary expense. He is in charge, and he is responsible for profits. More to the point, he knows his local situation.

In the ceaseless war on expense, that last point is vitally important. What may be brilliant strategy in one store may be nothing more than ill-advised penny-pinching in another. The size of the operation, its clientele, and its staff, all need to be considered.

Some Fundamentals

There are some fundamentals in expense control that are universal. One of these is that it should be made plain to the entire organization that top management wants waste minimized. If a branch manager sets a good example and responds warmly when employees cooperate, he is already on his way toward a workable program.

A second principle is that store-wide awareness and willingness to help should be encouraged. To this end, an occasional talk to supervisors or even the entire branch staff on the importance of saving pennies as well as dollars has its place. So have conferences with executives who head up selling and non-selling activities, and meetings with representatives of the rank-and-file. Campaigns and spot checks help, and suggestion boxes can make their contribution, too. Indifference, anywhere from the top down to the lowliest employee, is the worst enemy of expense control.

Another fundamental: Expense control is a year-round job. One suggestion is to assign someone to work at it every week of the year, so that this person becomes unusually aware of opportunities to save. Such a person can pick up an idea in one area and adapt it to the needs of another. In time, he will develop expertise.

Still another principle: Savings made in the name of expense control should be looked at from the store-wide viewpoint. There are times when one activity achieves expense reduction simply by shifting part of its responsibilities over to another. If the second department can absorb the work thrust upon it, the saving is genuine. But there can be cases where a thrifty manager cuts down in his own area and thus causes some other area to increase its costs by at least an offsetting amount.

Looking for Areas to Attack

Experts on expense control have urged branch managers to concentrate their efforts in those areas where substantial savings are likely to be achieved. Such areas show up clearly when the figures for a week or month or season are compared with those of the previous year. Any activity with an unduly large increase from one year to the next invites study.

Another suggested starting point is those taken-for-granted areas that are not regularly checked up on. Conditions at the branch may have changed, or new approaches may have developed. Meantime, the branch may be running along with its usual outlays for lights, telephone, or other services, let us say, instead of looking for ways to bring these costs down.

Some other general areas to investigate:

• Possible consolidations of jobs, functions, services.
• Possible purchase of machinery to reduce man-hours of labor, as in housekeeping activities and materials handling.
• Replacement of highly skilled help with less expensive help.

• Use of students, particularly those in retailing courses, as part-time help.

• Questioning of customer services, to reduce or eliminate those that seem not especially wanted, or to consider charging for some that have been given free, or increasing present charges.

• Standardization of forms and procedures wherever possible.

• Questioning of whatever is "always done this way," in search of a better way.

In some areas of attack, it may be necessary to call in an outside expert for advice. Often such help is available at no cost, as from the telephone company or from suppliers of cleaning materials and equipment. At other times, someone within the store organization, if not in the branch itself, may be expert and available—the executive in charge of a specific activity at the main store, for instance, or the manager of another branch that has already encountered a similar problem.

Specific Suggestions

Exchange of ideas on expense reduction is a favorite fare at NRMA Conventions—and possibly anywhere that retailers get together. Summarized below are suggestions that have been offered at past conventions by controllers, store operating heads, and others.

Those listed here have been selected for their applicability to the branch manager's job. Hundreds more are to be found in such NRMA publications as, "Successful Cost Cutting," by the Controllers' Congress; "Cutting Store Expense," by the Store Management Group; and "400 Ways to Reduce Expense," by the Store Management Group.

Suggestions are grouped under general topics. Using some of these to get discussion started at expense control meetings may bring forth a great many more.

Enlisting Cooperation

Require every manager of a selling or non-selling department to submit one expense-saving idea a month. Award prizes.

Set up an expense control committee for the branch. Schedule regular meetings and review possibilities and accomplishments.

Maintain a suggestion box. Use bulletin boards, store publication, or other medium to invite suggestions and to give recognition to contributors of useful ideas.

Occasionally, pick one area on which to concentrate—for instance, running a take-with campaign, or campaigning against errors on saleschecks. Give team and individual prizes.

Housekeeping and Maintenance

Keep a watchful eye on new equipment that can economically replace the hand broom, mop, or shovel. Gasoline powered sweepers, snow plows, and scrubbing machines, among others, can usually do the job in a fraction of the time needed by manpower and hand tools.

Standardize paint colors in non-selling areas as much as possible. Saves mixing-matching time; often saves second coat.

Make sure there is always a written schedule for cleaners to follow.

Electricity

Consider re-lamping and cleaning fixtures in blocks.

Make periodic check of wattages, especially in non-selling sections. Too much wattage adds to costs; too little may mean poor illumination and more errors.

Pay one or more employees a flat fee to go through the store quickly at closing time and turn off all switches that should be off for the night.

Tab light switches in various colors to indicate (1) those that should be on at all times, (2) those that should be turned on by the early shift of maids and porters, and (3) those that should be turned on just before the store opens.

One hour before closing, turn off the compressors of the air conditioning system, leaving only the blowers on for the final hour.

Display and Signing

Print signs on two sides of one card, instead of using two cards back to back.

Print signs without price. Gradually accumulate a stock of toppers that show prices, and use and re-use these as needed. Or purchase interchangeable price strips that can slip into holders wherever used in the store.

Cashiers

Leave coins in registers overnight; use them to start the day with.

Leave cash funds in registers overnight.

Use common cash drawers.

In Accounts Receivable, have slot where customers can deposit payments by check without waiting for receipt from cashier.

Restaurant hostess can double as cashier during slack periods.

Mail and Office

Cubby-holes for mail, at some central point or near service elevator on each floor, can eliminate desk-to-desk deliveries. Each secretary can bring her outgoing and interoffice mail to the central point and pick up her own department's incoming correspondence.

On minor letters, write the reply at the foot of the incoming letter, photocopy for the file, and mail the original. Some stores add a sticker on the virtues of such prompt but informal responses.

Look for opportunities to use form letters instead of individually dictated messages, printed forms instead of letters, postcards instead of letters.

Determine the maximum number of copies of a single message it is economical to make on photocopy machines. Post notice of method to be used if more than this quantity is required.

Delivery

Run occasional take-with drives.

Check registers at intervals to see if any one salesperson or department has exceptional proportion of delivery rather than take-with. Investigate.

When items are returned after purchase for repair by vendor, see if vendor can drop-ship the repaired item directly to customer.

When personalized merchandise is ordered, such as stationery or greeting cards, see if vendor can drop-ship directly to customer.

Workrooms

Consolidate men's and women's alterations.

Consolidate estimating work, as for interior decorating, floor coverings, and draperies, in one office.

Encourage alertness to salvage opportunities. Chipped mirrors can be cut down to smaller sizes; scrap lumber has many uses; waste cotton can pad chair arms.

Vocational school students make good part-time help. They bring motivation as well as skills to the job.

Make sure garment fitters are up to date on fashion details. Ignorance on this point can lead to alterations that spoil the look of the garment.

Keep reminding salespeople to sell the right size. Even if customer pays for the alteration, the store can lose money in trying to make the wrong size fit.

Workroom help can shift to gift-wrap, and gift-wrap girls can usually do simple sewing jobs in the workroom, according to the pressure of work.

Receiving, Marking, Transfers

Transfers made in sealed hampers can be opened, checked, and put into stock by the salespeople during slow periods.

On incoming parcel post shipments, require a notation of the value of postage used to be placed on the receiving apron, for comparison later with amount charged to store on the invoice.

Note and follow-up on any claims against vendors or carriers when merchandise comes directly to the branch. Consider non-marking of binned merchandise—recognizing that supervision and training are required to minimize errors in selling.

In marking merchandise that does not need table space, have salespeople affix the tickets during the early slow hours. This practice is not invariably recommended, however, because, without proper supervision, it can lead to shrinkage.

Stock Work

Pool all stock help under a supervisor who is experienced in this field, instead of assigning each stock person to individual departments.

Try to get deliveries into the store before opening, so that salespeople can put the goods in place during the quiet early hours.

When a stock man makes a delivery to a department, have him load any waiting "send" merchandise into his truck and take it to the delivery area on the return trip.

In departments like housewares, where many items are represented on the floor by samples only, set up an intercom to the stockroom, and have a stockboy bring out what is needed, instead of requiring the salesman to leave the floor.

Telephone and Telegraph

Review telephone installations annually, as in January of each year, for unneeded equipment—from call buttons to tie-lines. Do this with a telephone company representative, the main store's expert, or outside experts, who will know costs and have suggestions.

Investigate possibility of call distributors and private telephones to reduce load on switchboard.

Check or test-check all toll calls on the bill. Let it be known in the organization that such checking is done.

If direct outside dialing can be done from extensions, arrange for the telephone company operator to request the extension number on any calls beyond, say, five message units. The company will send monthly statements of the calls made, showing which extensions were used for each.

The psychological effect of the two procedures just above has been known to reduce bills noticeably.

Check on the possibility of replacing one or more of the full-time switchboard operators with part-timers.

Have all telegrams pass through hands of someone trained to minimize word count.

Vending Machines

If all are from one source, branch can have freer hand in choice of locations, and often a better deal.

Use food and drink machines in employee cafeteria for service before and after peak periods.

Christmas and Other Peaks

In areas that lend themselves to browse-and-buy shopping, consider the use of temporary check-out set-ups. Salespeople may be assigned to circulate within the area and assist customers, but the transactions can be written up at the check-out.

Use contingent salespeople for stock and receiving work early in the day, and early in their association with the department, until they are actually needed on the floor.

For positions that require special training, as in adjustments, try to recall people who have already done such work at your store, and who will thus be able to function effectively with a minimum of preparation.

Keep a list of good people for next year—both Christmas temporaries and retiring full-timers who no longer want year-round work.

Miscellaneous

Save the time of credit interviewers by letting customers fill out their own applications, and change-of-address forms. Exhibit blown-up samples as guides.

Consider alarm systems to substitute for some of the night watchmen.

In small stores, provide fill-in work for night watchman to do between rounds—coin counts, for instance.

In large stores, provide electric cart so that one watchman can cover greater area.

Replace or supplement nurse by having one or more qualified first-aiders on each shift. For stores open many hours, the few extra dollars added to the first aiders' pay will probably cost less than additional nurse time.

Consider part-time use of wrapping personnel, letting clerks do the wrapping in slow hours.

Consolidate several customer conveniences in one location, with fewer clerks: accommodation desk, gift wrap, and lost and found, for instance.

Be alert to waste in use of supplies. Remind salespeople to use smallest box or bag for each purchase; one paper carry handle for a package; one-side seals on folding boxes, etc. Run occasional drives and clinics on this subject.

Consider a washing machine for laundering mops, cloths, and work uniforms.

Occasionally check prices and quantities of sanitary supplies, cleaning supplies, etc., if purchased at branch.

Arrange employee vacation schedules with regard to peaks and valleys in the employee's own work, rather than store sales peaks.

CHAPTER 19

CONTROLLING STOCK SHORTAGES

When the stock shortage figure for a branch is climbing upward, the manager can be pretty sure that his own prestige with management is heading in the opposite direction. Shortages not only destroy profits; they also destroy management's confidence in the supervision at the branch.

It behooves the branch manager, therefore, to do all he can to keep shortages under control. There are many things he can do—with emphasis upon "many." Shortages have no one cause and no one cure. Only a many-pronged and continuing program can keep them under control.

Causes of shortage fall into three classes: (1) actual loss, as through theft of goods or cash; (2) inaccurately taken inventories, as through wrong counts or calculations; (3) inaccuracies in systems and procedures, as through failure to enter a markdown, over-rings and under-rings on cash registers, errors in counts, prices, and extensions on receipts, transfers, markdowns, and other documents. The more care that is taken in these last two areas, the smaller the chances of loss in the first one.

The branch manager's own attitude is the starting point. He himself must demonstrate and insist upon careful adherence to system if he wishes to avoid laxity on the part of subordinates.

His personal example and continuing efforts can make his entire staff accuracy-conscious. Departments and classifications that show good figures or marked improvement should get special praise from him personally. Those that appear to be running into trouble should get all the help he can give them toward solving their problems.

Stock shortages, of course, are nothing new in retailing. Many merchants have had to deal with the problem, and many experts have been called in for advice. From the talks and articles of such merchants and consultants, the following list of suggestions has been compiled.

Not all the items on the check-list will apply to any one branch, but almost any branch manager will find a few ideas he can put to work at once. The list, then, is a starting point, from which an individual branch's shortage prevention program can grow.

The Branch Manager

Set up an inventory shortage committee to help study trouble spots and improve the overall performance.

Give at least one executive the permanent assignment of looking into causes and cures of shortages, both to locate weak spots and to maintain interest in continued improvement.

Educate department managers to their responsibility for shortage control.

Invite suggestions from sales-supporting executives.

Discuss shortage problem with entire staff. Invite suggestions. Solicit cooperation. Explain that shortages reflect on everyone. Hold meetings, storewide and for small groups of employees, to air the problem.

Check weekly sales and stock reports to make sure your branch has been correctly credited with its sales, and has been charged only with shipments actually received. Where there are several branches, one's banner day receipts are sometimes put on another's record.

Make sure every new employee knows his duties and knows where to turn for help and advice. Error prevention starts here!

Invite main store protection chief to consult with branch manager and protection staff on problem areas.

Make spot checks throughout the branch to see how stock and

paper work are handled—and to let employees know that management wants things done properly.

Insist on observance of check-passing rules.

In any area of known weakness—plant, system, or people—make frequent and obvious checks until the problem can be brought under better control. Make mid-season inventories in departments with high shrinkage.

If there is reason to suspect after-hours thefts, go over lighting, alarms, locks, etc., with branch protection chief, main store's protection manager, and/or local police official. Consider use of undercover agents, stake-outs, etc.

Under no circumstances condone infractions of shortage-prevention rules, even on the part of otherwise valuable employees.

Never consider the job or any part of it finished. This is a continuing responsibility.

At Inventory Time

Talk to entire staff on importance of accuracy. Insist that instructions from controller's office be followed explicitly.

Review instructions at staff meeting. During inventory taking, circulate among departments and question people to be sure that all is clear. Being personally in evidence during the proceedings serves the additional function of giving encouragement to the conscientious and discouraging back-sliding by the slipshod.

Require each department manager to circulate similarly.

Check deliveries, invoice dates, transfers, returns, etc., to make sure cut-off date is uniformly observed.

When Goods Are Received at Branch

Allow no one in checking area who is not working there.

Have the person who opens a carton do the counting of its contents.

Have clerks check seals on interstore transfers and condition of vendor shipments before they are opened.

Be no less conscientious in checking interstore transfers than in checking vendor shipments. Both are subject to error and possible theft if lax procedures creep in.

Report shortages, overages, and damages at once. If vendor is responsible, make out chargeback, or request buyer to do so. If shipment is inter-store, notify sending unit and make out chargeback.

If claims and chargebacks have to be made out at the main store, follow up to make sure this has been done.

Verify all prices, specifications, and department numbers, in addition to quantities.

Require invoices to be signed and checked promptly.

Check at intervals to make sure merchandise is not left exposed, that outsiders are not permitted to enter, etc.

When Marking Is Done at Branch

Allow no one into marking area who does not work there.

Lock marking room when not in use.

Assign control of price tickets to responsible individual.

Require markers to check counts and verify prices and department numbers on each lot.

Use marking personnel to make or supervise price changes in stock. Require them to check quantity, former price, new price, against markdown or other document covering the price changes.

If sales people are used for re-marking, insist upon effective supervision, checking of counts, and accurate reporting.

Make sure marking room has adequate space and facilities. Overcrowding leads to errors.

Check the counting and marking occasionally, to encourage meticulous care.

Provide security cages for receiving and marking pilferable items, such as guns, jewelry, drugs, furs.

For Department Managers

Insist on orderly stockrooms.

Allow no one in stockroom who does not have business there.

Keep pilferable articles in locked stockrooms. For items like jewelry, locked showcases may be set up in selling areas.

Check non-marked merchandise for proper signing and/or binning on selling floor.

When price tags become detached from goods in stock, verify the price before permitting new tickets to be attached.

Do all paper work on merchandise movement, price changes, breakage immediately. Delay breeds errors and oversights.

Record all loans of merchandise to display or other departments. Follow up for return.

When merchandise is sent to vendor or main store to be repaired or replaced, make out a chargeback or transfer. The item can be re-billed or re-transferred when it comes back to the branch.

Let it be understood that a high shortage figure may adversely affect the department manager's chances of pay increases and promotion.

Employee Hiring and Supervision

Screen all employees before they report for work. A quick credit check is a good investment. Be just as careful with part-timers as with full-time employees. Test check employment practice and records at intervals.

Be more—not less—careful of Easter and Christmas extras. These people will be working when supervision is at its weakest.

Be alert for any personality or personal problems among employees that make them more than ordinarily prone to error or temptation.

Promptly fire anyone caught in dishonesty. Whether or not the store publicizes the case, make sure the loophole that made theft possible is plugged.

Restrict employee entrances and exits to a single door.

Provide lockers for employees' coats and purses near their door. Spot check the contents at intervals.

Employee packages should be systematically inspected. Ideally, they should be brought to the door well ahead of closing time, so that all can be inspected and checked. If complete daily inspection is impossible, every tenth or twentieth package should be inspected each day, or days should be selected at irregular intervals for inspection of all packages.

Require gift-wrap desk to check sales slips before wrapping employee purchases.

Keep a log book for all who enter or leave the building after hours, including porters and cleaners.

Call supervisors to account, as well as their subordinates, for infractions of shortage control rules by rank-and-file people.

Exits and Entrances

Keep strict control of keys. Require them to be returned to a keyboard each day.

Master keys, if any, should be held only by top executives.

Consider installing bells on side doors and other emergency exits to discourage theft.

Cash Registers

Place all registers in plain sight.

Check any register, or work shift, or individual salesperson with too many overages or shortages. Overages sometimes indicate cash thefts have been imperfectly concealed by under-ringing sales. Give recognition to employees or departments with top accuracy records.

Check if the percentage of cash to charge sales is consistently lower than store or department average. Some cash sales may not have been registered.

Check for consistently high "No sale" rings. Discourage change-making from the register as an accommodation. A special accommodation desk should take care of this service.

Require register drawers to be closed after each transaction.

Insist upon error-prevention routine at the register: (1) Ring up each sale separately and at once. (2) Call the amount due and the amount received. (3) Make change and complete the transaction, giving a receipt, before wrapping the merchandise.

In departments where there is much self-service and sales-people spend most of their time at the registers, be sure the registers are placed so that even a short saleswoman has a good view of what goes on in the department.

Insist on observance of check-passing rules.

Customer Returns and Allowances

Require executive approval of returns made without ticket and sales slip. These may be shoplifted goods. In doubtful cases, offer to mail customer a refund check.

Teach and re-teach cash refund procedures.

Spot check authenticity of refunds by sending a "What did we do wrong?" letter to a sample of refund recipients. Investigate if more than two or three per cent of the letters prove undeliverable.

Keep tight control on cash refund forms.

Salesbooks

Keep careful control of salesbooks. Require stub of old one before issuing the new.

Spot-check tallies and sales checks, especially where there is interselling, to guard against credits to wrong departments.

Maintain continuous pressure for accuracy, particularly on charge-takes. Run anti-error campaigns, with awards to individuals and teams with fewest errors.

Salespeople vs. Shoplifters

Teach and re-teach system and security routine.

Stage accuracy contests among salespeople. Anti-error campaigns discourage theft as well as carelessness.

Educate salespeople on value of merchandise, so that they will be less vulnerable to the shoplifter device of switched price tickets.

Emphasize importance of a prompt greeting or approach. Customers like the attention; shoplifters are discouraged by it.

Employee discounts—for accuracy of rate and calculations.

Price tickets—for legibility and correctness.

Non-marked merchandise—for proper binning and signing.

Housekeeping—to be sure nothing about a merchandise department indicates the sloppiness that invites shoplifting.

Workroom—to be sure procedures do not encourage damage or pilferage.

Conclusion

This list is only a beginning, but in stock shortage control, the important thing is to begin. Then, having begun, to keep at it forever after. This is one field in which complacency leads to disaster.

CHAPTER 20

MAINTAINING BRANCH SECURITY

Branch security presents a many-sided problem, some phases of which have been discussed in the chapters on shortage, expense, and housekeeping, among others. Here, however, is a check-list that touches all aspects of the problem. It is the work of Harvey Burstein, Harvey Burstein Consultants Corporation, Valley Stream, New York. Mr. Burstein presented this summary of the security job at an NRMA Branch Store Institute.

Physical Security

Grounds (suburban) with or without parking facilities. Where possible consider use of heavy shrubs as security fencing, leaving openings only where required for direct access; also use as divider between parking areas and building.

Parking facilities. Minimize direct access between parking areas and building proper. No direct access from parking areas to shipping and receiving areas. After hours illumination.

Exterior lighting. Perimeter lighting throughout hours of darkness; protect lights against vandalism.

Exterior doors. Burglar-proof locks; key controls; alarms for "closed" periods.

Interior doors. Burglar-proof locks, avoid use of master keys; key controls; alarms for sensitive areas.

Emergency exits only. Always secured with alarmed, approved fire locks; keys controlled.

Display windows. Shatter-proof glass; alarmed for "closed" periods.

Merchandise displays. Avoid displays of a height that obscures the vision of sales and/or protection personnel; avoid displays of expensive merchandise in close proximity to doors to street; keep small, expensive items in showcases, preferably locked when not in use.

Key and locks. Avoid needless use of master and sub-master keys; use locks with changeable cores; where padlocks are used, use those with changeable combinations; avoid exposed screwheads on hasps; take steps to minimize risk of unauthorized key duplication.

Mirrors. Use strategically located mirrors to assist sales and protection personnel in covering areas not directly in line of sight.

Closed circuit television. Consider use for coverage of shipping and receiving areas; also for particularly vulnerable selling areas and means of ingress and egress to and from the store.

Storage facilities (merchandise). Enclose stock rooms with floor to ceiling barriers and full doors (dutch type); lock stock room doors when area unattended; keep top open and lower half secured during operation; use locked or sealed spivies for intrastore and inter-store transportation whenever possible.

Locker rooms. Locate as near employee entrance-exist as possible with minimum passage through stock or sales areas.

Personnel office. Locate near store entrance, if possible; avoid placement in "heart" of store.

Payroll, accounting and executive offices. Locate away from entrances, preferably on upper floors of multi-storied building otherwise near "core" of building.

Time clocks. Locate between locker rooms and employee exit, nearer the latter than the former.

Stock rooms. Locate in single area if possible, preferably near receiving entrance; separate stock room for each department.

Shipping and receiving office. Abutting shipping and receiving platforms with unobstructed view of interior and exterior.

Dressing rooms. On edge of department using; single access to area; arrange to facilitate observation of individual units by sales personnel and/or checkers.

Sales areas. See "Merchandise Displays." Avoid crowding departments together with very narrow aisles; when possible have bulky items closer to exits than smaller and more expensive ones (better costume jewelry, furs, better dresses, etc.) with latter in more centralized locations.

Administrative or Operational Security

Employment practices. Adequately detailed applications for all jobs and all periods accounted for; thorough interviews; credit checks; physical examinations, verify former employment with previous employers and supervisors; verify background data via references; anticipate needs and avoid "crash" hiring programs; conduct orientation programs for all new personnel and include discussion of protection; issue color coded name tags and identification cards to all employees.

Payroll practices. Make all payments by check; give check only to payee unless another is authorized by him in writing to pick up same; consider possible use of payroll deductions for employee purchases.

Employee purchases. Limit hours for all employee purchases; if employee discount extended to family, restrict both degree of relationship and hours, insist upon show of employee identification when purchases made and note identifying number on sales check (can "imprint" if charge-a-plate type plastic ID card used); purchases to be taken instead of sent to be kept in selling department until collected for distribution at time of departure; employee purchase records to be spot checked periodically for unusual purchases or patterns.

Employee entrances and exits. All personnel to enter and depart via designated doors at all times and same to be under some form of "supervision" at all times; no employee to enter before prescribed time, or to remain beyond a fixed hour, with written authorization of the department head or store manager.

Locker rooms. All personal clothing and other personal property to be kept in assigned lockers; no personal property, including purses, to be carried on the floor or in stock rooms (management may issue small clear plastic "purses" for the convenience of female employees); locker rooms to be used only upon arrival at or departure from the store, not during the working day.

Stock rooms. Locked when unattended; no unauthorized personnel allowed when open; use lower half dutch door as a counter when receiving or releasing merchandise; not to be used as substitute locker or lunch rooms; no merchandise issued without written order signed by someone at "supervisory" level; keys turned in end of each day.

Dressing rooms. Limit number of garments allowed any one person at any one time (possible maximum of 3); check customer parcels before allowing them into the dressing rooms; rooms to be kept clean, checked frequently and regularly; consider use of a checker or clerk and "tags" in "reception" area of dressing room units.

Shipping and receiving. Keep platforms clear; do not allow truckers beyond platforms and/or office; use pre-numbered forms for all outgoing shipments with all of the numbers to be accounted for; all deliveries to be counted upon receipt and before movement to stock areas.

Key and combination controls. Keys and combinations to be made available solely on the basis of necessity, not of convenience or status; person knowing combination no longer needs same, change combination; do not issue grand master keys to anyone; if possible keep accurate records on all keys issued; keys to be returned when no longer required for job; if keys lost or lock tampered with, change lock core or cylinder.

Inter and intra-store shipments. Use closed, locked shipping containers whenever possible; lock or seal trucks and/or spivies in inter-store shipments, unlocking or breaking of seals to be by authorized personnel only, count all merchandise upon receipt, not only by receiving personnel but also by stock room personnel before placing in stock; ship only on the basis of written orders.

Mark-ups and mark-downs. To be handled by specifically designated persons only; all entries to be made daily and no allowed exceptions; records to be inspected regularly for current status and accuracy.

Inventory practices. Complete inventory at least annually; complete inventory of each department (rotation basis) at least twice a year; permanent inventories most helpful, inventories not taken by departmental personnel and to be supervised by representative of controller's staff; all major discrepancies to be checked out, others to be pursued on a selective basis.

Cash refunds. To be made at departmental level; merchandise to be carefully examined to insure that it is in fact sold at the store; no cash refunds without written approval of department head or specifically designated assistant.

Cash pick-ups. All "surplus" cash from registers to be picked up during the day on a regular but non-routine basis; collected monies to be picked up in locked receptacles; no cash left in registers over night; each employee to have own "bank" and to tally daily.

Sales personnel. Keep all stock in orderly manner; remove empty hangers at all times; replace merchandise on racks, in piles, etc. as soon as it has served its purpose if not sold; cooperate and do not wait for person who has shown merchandise and who still is busy to finish with customer and straighten stock; prompt and courteous attention to every potential customer; be alert; cooperate with Protection Department; close cash registers after each transaction; each employee to have own register number, and drawer if possible.

Janitorial and maintenance personnel. Do all or bulk of work during day; closely supervised at all times; know whereabouts at all times; periodic spot checks by managerial personnel more especially if working in store after closing.

Visitors from main store or other branches. Use employee entrance-exit; identify themselves; same treatment as store personnel if departing with packages (unless departing before end of day when verification of merchandise is based upon examination of contents versus sales slip).

Protection Department

Size. Allow for full time, daily coverage; no quick come-backs; 2 consecutive days off per week; supervisory and secretarial-clerical help; review requirements annually to avoid over or under staffing.

Qualifications. Physically fit, high school graduate, good manners and appearance; no derogatory credit or criminal information; military or prior security experience helpful but not necessary; same regarding retail experiences; capable of passing full field investigation.

Training. Program specially designed for retailing to be given at time of appointment, no exceptions; emphasis on firm but polite conduct; problems of shoplifting and employee theft; police and fire liaison.

Supervision. Qualified supervisor with good understanding of retailing plus protection; spot checks of all protection personnel while on duty; emphasis on prevention rather than detection and apprehension; understand role as part of management team; have sub-supervisory personnel available.

Budget. Be realistic; allow for base pay, fringes, shift differential, etc., replacement of equipment; if special requests received from specific department for personnel, "charge" their budget on a reimbursable basis.

Authority. Statement of store policy; duties and responsibilities outlined. Consider deputizing; legal authority, deputized or otherwise.

Assignments. Plain clothes. Rotate posts and shifts.

Communications. Two-way radio; reports; forms (complaint, incident, accident, etc.).

Patrols. Around the clock; interior and exterior; avoid patterns; check-in to insure proper coverage.

Emergency planning. Fire; flood; riot; tornado, earthquake.

Police and fire liaison. Close cooperation; personal contact Protection Managers, Precinct Commander and local fire Battalion Chief.

Miscellaneous. Liaison with Main Store Protection Department; liaison with other retail store Protection Managers, cooperation at store level among protection, personnel, purchasing managers.

CHAPTER 21

BRANCH MAINTENANCE
AND HOUSEKEEPING

One of the most valuable properties entrusted to the branch manager is the building that houses the operation he supervises. Owned or rented, it requires careful preventive maintenance to keep repair costs within bounds. And, owned or rented, it demands housekeeping of the most meticulous kind. Customer good will, employee attitudes, the safety of people and merchandise, all depend on how well these two functions are handled.

Maintenance

Good maintenance embraces a great deal more than calling a contractor in to refinish the roof or parking lot, or to replace a damaged door or window. It involves taking care of the store plant so as to prevent unnecessary wear and, as far as possible, to avoid breakdowns of such systems as heating, ventilating, and transportation. It involves also thinking ahead to possible emergencies and preparing for them.

Preventive Maintenance

Preventive maintenance, like preventive medicine, aims to ward off breakdowns by regular inspection and servicing. In the modern store, there are many machines that need such inspection, from typewriters to heating plants. One can no longer expect a handyman or even a mechanical engineer to have the diversified know-how to be able to service them all. Locating dependable agencies to inspect and service each of the various types of equipment within a branch is no easy task, particularly in a suburb whose main purpose is merely to provide living room for growing families. Therefore, a high priority should be given to the task of working up a list of experts, in and out of the store, whose combined efforts will keep the branch's equipment in running order.

Compiling such a list may require correspondence with the makers whose products have been installed in the branch, or a study of the local telephone directory, or consultation with the main store, or a canvass of branch employees for recommendations. Or all of these!

Once compiled, the entire list should be readily available to the branch manager and his assistant. Appropriate sections of it should be posted (and kept up to date) for any employees who are authorized to schedule service and repair calls of any kind. The night watchman, for instance, may need a list of people to call in the event of heat or power failure, or the office supervisor may need the list of typewriter, adding machine, and register repair firms.

Once compiled, however, the list should not be regarded as sacred. A sensible idea is to maintain the branch manager's version on cards, at least 5 x 8 in size, so that there is room for corrections and comments. Such comments could include a brief summary of the terms and the renewal date of the contract, and any remarks about the promptness and efficiency of the service.

Since much service work is done on a contract basis, a wise plan is to set up a tickler file, so that the branch manager is reminded well in advance of those contracts that will soon come up for renewal. Thus he allows himself time to check into prices, service, and possible changes before the new contract date is upon him. Equipment that lends itself to such treatment includes: Air conditioning, alteration room machines, boilers, cash registers, elevators, escalators, office machines, and refrigerators, among others.

Standby Equipment

In some instances, machinery much used at the branch would cause severe disruption and expense if it were out of service. A possible trouble preventive is to have a stand-by machine, to be used while the vital equipment is under repair. The stand-by may be an older model, or it may be a spare that the main store keeps available for any of the branches that may face an emergency. If a stand-by is available, information as to its whereabouts should be readily accessible in the branch manager's office and, in some instances, also in the work area where the need may occur.

Typical items for which stand-by equipment may prove valuable include: typewriters, registers, adding machines, vacuum cleaners and other basic housekeeping tools, alteration equipment, marking machines.

In judging when an investment in stand-by equipment is wise, consider the cost of the item (used or new), the availability or nonavailability of nearby repair service, the cost in time and service of being without the equipment, the probable length of time it would be out of service for repair, the possibility of renting a substitute or borrowing one during the repair period, the space available in which to store a spare, and similar factors.

Disaster Conditions

Every organization, including a branch, has to prepare to cope with large and small emergencies that are completely unrelated to its normal business. For each of these contingencies, instructions should be formulated in advance, so that confusion and possible loss of life or merchandise is prevented. For example:

Fire. Even when fire prevention is preached and taught, fires can occur. Instructions should be formulated and taught as to

- turning in the alarm
- containing the blaze, if possible
- protecting the merchandise
- evacuating personnel and customers.

The locations of alarm boxes and extinguishers should be taught on an employee's first day. Extinguishers should be inspected regularly. Alarms should have regularly scheduled tests. Evacuation procedures should be worked out, taught, and reviewed regularly.

Local fire officials are usually pleased to address employees on fire prevention and on what to do in case of fire.

First Aid. If the branch has no nurse on the premises, first aid training should be given to several people on each floor. Part of this training should be in how to report an accident, so that the store is protected from exaggerated damage claims. A good source of advice on this and all safety subjects is the company handling the store's liability insurance. Such companies are usually equipped to send qualified experts into the stores to inspect, advise, and instruct.

Snow and Storm. Standing instructions, reviewed at intervals, should be given for action in the event of snow or storm conditions that constitute a hazard to travel or store safety. If snow removal is contracted for, the name and telephone of the party who handles the store's work should be posted in the branch manager's office and at the desk of any aide he authorizes to order the work in his absence.

Throughout the winter months, if the branch is in a cold climate, supervisors should be required to maintain lists of nearby personnel who will fill in for absentees when travel is difficult.

"Battle stations" should be assigned for inspecting roofs, drains, and other areas likely to cause trouble under prolonged storm conditions.

One or more persons should have the responsibility for checking walks and parking area for icy conditions and arranging to have the spots sanded promptly.

Blackouts. If the branch has its own generator as standby power in the event of electrical current failure, several responsible people should know how to make the switch. Every supervisor should know where to find emergency lanterns, candles, or flashlights. Advance preparation for power failure is especially important in windowless or nearly windowless store buildings, so that the dangers of panic and looting are minimized.

Safety Team. Individuals who seem calm and intelligent can be recruited into a safety team, whose members will be prepared to take the initiative in the event of any emergency. Training of such teams can be done by lecture, discussion, or distribution of literature. Sources of help are: main store's safety director, local police and fire officials, Red Cross, protection head, insurance companies.

Special Emergencies

Conditions as varied as transit strikes or special sales may cause enormous congestion in the branch's parking lot. Preparation in advance can include a roof or other elevated watch position for a traffic director, who can use a walkie-talkie to help the guards on the ground handle the flow of vehicles. If the branch is in a shopping center, the center management may take on this responsibility at the store's suggestion.

Other emergencies: If the branch's business shows signs of outgrowing its plant, outside storage possibilities should be investigated before the need becomes acute: trailers, tents, inflatable (air bubble) shells supported by compressed air, etc. Additional protection staff may be needed when such devices are used—but the cost will probably be less than the cost of being short of merchandise.

Store Modernization

Branch managers tend to regard store design as a fact of life, to be accepted and lived with. Many store heads, however, make a point of consulting their branch managers before building a new branch or enlarging present buildings. A branch head may not be an architect or store planner, but his day-to-day activities make him more likely than the professionals to be able to put his finger on problems and opportunities in store design. His is the practical view of the man who lives with the end product.

If branches of the future are to be better planned than those of the past, each branch manager should prepare himself to pass his suggestions, fully documented, along to management when the opportunity presents itself. His suggestions may range from the need for more receiving and marking space to a request for employee locker rooms, a community meeting room, or an air conditioning system with capacity adequate for days of peak customer traffic.

Although he himself may not have a ready solution, the branch manager can put his problems on the table, constructively, with indications of how improvements can be expected to yield improved volume, reduced markdowns, better employee morale, reduced expense, or whatever the case may be. Some of the wanted improvements may add to the costs of building the next branch, or of modernizing and expanding the present one. With the information the branch manager supplies, his firm's management will be able to weigh the added costs against the possibility of enhanced profits, and reach a sounder decision than might otherwise be handed down.

Branch Housekeeping *

Housekeeping is probably one of the most poorly organized and wastefully executed functions in the retail world. It need not be. There are simple, sensible approaches to follow that will keep costs in line and yet produce a cleaner, more secure retail plant. Much of what needs to be done to put these procedures into effect is, fortunately, within the scope of the branch manager's authority.

Management's Responsibility

Management's (or the branch manager's) first step toward getting a better housekeeping job is to assign an executive to study and head up this function.

The man or woman chosen should be of sufficient stature to

---

* The housekeeping section of this chapter has drawn heavily upon the NRMA Store Management Group's "Housekeeping Manual for Retail Stores." Prepared by three experts in the field, it contains forms, charts, and procedures that will prove invaluable to anyone undertaking the responsibility for getting the most out of his store's housekeeping dollar. The price is $10 a copy to NRMA members, with a reduction for additional copies. Non-members pay more.

work with other management executives in developing a clear idea of what is to be done, how many people will be needed, and at what cost. He or she should be capable of assessing and explaining the need for purchasing equipment or hiring outside contractors, whenever either of these courses suggests itself as desirable and economical.

Management, in the person of the branch manager, also has the further responsibility of inculcating a respect for the housekeeping job among the rest of the store staff. Tidiness should be insisted upon at each person's desk or other work station. The easy habit of taking porters and maids off their assigned duties to run errands or do unassigned chores should be discouraged, unless allowance is made for the time so used when housekeeping budgets and personnel requirements are set up.

Measuring the Job

The housekeeping job should be measured—literally. Each floor should be divided into sections on a rough plan, and each section should be labeled as to its department number and area in square feet. Outside areas, entrances, escalators, offices, lavatories, and other special facilities for employees or customers should be similarly measured and labeled.

With this floor plan, however crudely drafted, the executive in charge is ready to take an inventory of the housekeeping tasks for which his staff is responsible.

For the selling departments, offices, and non-selling areas, in total, he lists the number of square feet of floor area to be cleaned, using a separate line for each type of flooring. He lists also the square footage of wall space, listing opaque sections separately from those that use clear glass, since each needs different cleaning methods and frequency. Display fixtures are similarly listed, with the glass surfaces separately from the opaque. Windows (other than display) are listed; light fixtures; the number of fitting rooms; the number of desks in each office.

Similar inventories are made at entrances, showing the floors, walls, doors, and light fixtures to be kept clean. For each display

Example of Standard Cleaning Method

MACHINE CONDITIONING — FLOORS

PURPOSE: To protect soft resilient floors from unnecessary wear and give them a lustre.

TYPES OF FLOOR: Large open areas of asphalt tile, rubber tile, vinyl and linoleum; and all sealed hardwood floors.

UNIT TIME ESTIMATE: 1½ man-hours per 1,000 square feet.

EQUIPMENT AND SUPPLIES:

- Floor machine and polishing brush.
- No. 3 steel wool pads.
- Floor conditioner—water emulsion natural paste wax (particularly applicable in this method of floor conditioning).
- Sheen-treated dust mop.

Basic Steps

1. *Preparation*
   - Machine conditioning is usually preceded by Standard Cleaning Method No. 1—Machine Stripping—Floors, and the area is already prepared for floor conditioning. When applied to sealed hardwood floors, this method is usually preceded by Standard Cleaning Method No. 8—Wet Mopping—Floors.

2. *Apply the Conditioner*
   - Place about 2 ounces of the floor conditioner on the center of the steel wool pad and run the machine over a small area to lubricate the pad.
   - Place another 2 ounces of conditioner on the pad and apply a first coat to an area of about 25 square feet and continue running the machine until the floor appears dry.
   - Place another 2 ounces on the pad and apply a second coat to the same area.
   - Continue applying 2 coats to each 25 square foot area until the entire floor is completed.

3. *Buff the Floor*
   - Slowly buff the floor with a polishing brush.

4. *Dust Mop the Floor*
   - Dust mop the entire floor with the sheen-treated dust mop, following Standard Cleaning Method No. 4—Dust Mopping—Floors.

5. *Follow-Up*
   - For asphalt tile, rubber tile, vinyl and linoleum buff the floor daily for the next 10 days. Then follow up daily with Standard Cleaning Method No. 3—Machine Reconditioning—Floors.
   - For sealed hardwood floors follow up approximately twice a year with Standard Cleaning Method No. 3.

Reprinted with permission from "Housekeeping Manual for Retail Stores," NRMA, 1963; p 73

EXHIBIT 23

window, the inside and outside glass areas are separately shown, since the outer surfaces will need frequent cleaning, but the inner ones will be cleaned only when displays are changed and no merchandise is in the way.

Wash rooms are listed, with details of the number and kind of facilities in each. Vertical transportation elements are listed, with details as to units and landings.

Example of form for Cleaning Inventory and Man Hour Requirements
Sales Departments, Offices and Non-Selling Areas

Floor _____   Department _____

Inventory — Major Items	Square Foot Area	Daily	Week	Bi-Week	Month	Bi-Month	Quarter	½-Year	Annual
1. Floors–Type 1									
2									
3									
2. Walls and Partitions Opaque Surfaces									
Glass Surfaces									
3. Windows (Other Than Display)									
4. Light Fixtures Covers or Diffusers									
5. Display Fixtures Glass Surfaces									
Opaque Surfaces									
6. Fitting Rooms Number of Units									
7. Office Furniture Number of Desks									

Total Man Hour Requirements

Major Items (Above)			
Minor Items			
Daily Periodic Servicing			
Department Total			

Reprinted with permission from "Housekeeping Manual for Retail Stores,"
NRMA, 1963; p 20

EXHIBIT 24

Estimating Man-Hours

For each of these inventories of major items to be kept clean, the time required will be calculated. To do this, there must first be an estimate of the man-hours required for the job. And, in turn, before the man-hours can be estimated, standards must be set up for the cleaning wanted, and the tools, supplies, and procedures to be used.

This is a quite different approach from turning a crew of untrained, unskilled workers loose to do a job, with minimum instructions and with no idea of how much is expected of them.

Substantial help is available in working out the procedures, equipment, supplies, and man-hours needed on specific jobs. Manufacturers of equipment and supplies can offer a good deal of help. The NRMA "Housekeeping Manual" on which this chapter is based lists such information for various jobs and suggests, for example, one and one-half man-hours per 1,000 square feet of floor space to be machine conditioned (polished); or one-tenth of a man-hour for dust-mopping an open area of that size, and two-tenths of a man-hour for dust-mopping a congested area of 1,000 square feet.

The man-hour estimates from outside sources provide a starting place. Actual experience may show the time required in the branch to be more or less than the typical. Experience may also show improvement in performance, as skills are acquired and as better equipment is brought into play. Continuing study and test-checking should be encouraged by the branch manager.

Deciding When to Clean

Deciding how often and how thoroughly each area will be cleaned is a matter of establishing priorities in the light of conditions at the branch.

The NRMA "Housekeeping Manual" suggests priorities to be assigned to various areas, and the frequencies with which cleaning tasks should be done under each priority. The suggestions cover

Example of Procedures, Frequencies, and Unit Time Estimates For
Routine Cleaning of General Housekeeping Items

Item	Procedure	Unit Time Estimates (Man-Hours)
Office Furniture	DAILY: Trash removal, dusting of furniture and accessories	
	WEEKLY: Spot-cleaning and dusting of furniture surfaces, window sills and baseboards	¼ per group of 5 desks
	WEEKLY: Vacuuming of drapes, venetian blinds and upholstered furniture when carpet or rug is done	
Toilet Rooms	DAILY: Empty and wipe waste disposal containers; wipe down walls, doors, partitions, etc.; damp clean mirrors; wash basins and hardware; scour inside of toilet bowls and urinals, wipe off outside surfaces; replace dispenser supplies; wet mop floors	¼ per 5 basic units (commodes, urinals, wash-basins)
	DAILY SERVICING: 3 times a day spot clean walls and floors, damp wipe basins and mirrors, empty waste receptacles, replace dispenser supplies	*
Elevators	DAILY: Dust and spot-clean all surfaces, wash glass on signs, wet mop floor	¼ per elevator car
	MONTHLY: Wash all surfaces within and adjacent to elevator; polish metal; strip and condition floor	2 per car
	DAILY SERVICING: 3 times a day dust mop floors and spot clean all surfaces	*
Stairways	DAILY: Dust hand rails, window sills and other items on stairwall within easy reach; dust mop stairway; remove gum, etc. with putty knife; spot clean doors, walls, steps and risers	1/10 per flight of approx. 15 steps, 4 feet wide
	WEEKLY: Wet mop	
	DAILY SERVICING: Approximately 3 times a day pick up papers and other waste items, spot-clean marks and spillage	*

*Store's estimate depending upon amount of Daily Servicing required.

Reprinted with permission from "Housekeeping Manual for Retail Stores;" NRMA, 1963; p 71

EXHIBIT 25

both daily cleaning and servicing needed to keep an area in constant orderliness (maintenance cleaning) and the periodic heavy duty cleaning (general cleaning) such as stripping heavy grime from floors and refinishing them.

Both the downtown store and its suburban branches may agree that sales departments should get top priority; offices, medium; and out-of-sight work areas, low. The frequency with which the actual cleaning is done under each priority will vary, however. The dust and traffic in the downtown store may require offices to be wall-dusted monthly, whereas a suburban branch may not have to dust office walls more often than once every two or three months, or even annually.

On the other hand, salespeople in the downtown store may be able to keep glass shelves and showcases presentably clean for long periods without the help of the housekeeping staff. In the suburban store, where mothers are likely to be accompanied by small children, the finger-mark accumulation may be quite rapid, and require more frequent attention from the cleaners.

Each branch's housekeeping head should familiarize himself with such points of difference for his unit, and should adjust the priorities and frequencies he assigns to that unit's needs.

It is important to impress upon the housekeeping head that priorities and frequencies suggested by outside sources, including the main store, are simply starting points. He should be reminded to review his program constantly, in order to eliminate excessive servicing and provide additional goings-over where they are needed.

Budgeting Man-Hours

When priorities have been set for all areas, and when procedures and estimated man-hours have been worked out for every cleaning operation (no small tasks!), the executive in charge of housekeeping is ready to work toward a budget.

He goes back now to his inventory of housekeeping items. On each list, he sets up columns for the jobs to be done daily, weekly, or at whatever less frequent intervals apply. For areas like selling departments and offices, he may have daily tasks, weekly, bi-weekly, monthly, bi-monthly, quarterly, semi-annual, and annual assignments. For display windows, he may have simply a daily requirement to wipe down the outside surface and a monthly requirement to wash both inner and outer surfaces.

His estimates of the man-hours required are made in terms of the units on his inventory—square feet for most things, but not all. Wash rooms are estimated on the basis of the number of facilities; elevators, escalators, and stairs, in terms of number of each, landings to be serviced, etc. If there are minor tasks to be performed

Example of Form of Housekeeping Personnel Requirements

Frequency	Cleaning Man Hour Requirements Per Frequency	Utility Service Man Hour Requirements Per Frequency	Total Man Hour Requirements Per Frequency	Annual Man Hour Requirements	
				Conversion Factor	Man Hours
Daily				x 310 Days	
Week				x 52 Weeks	
Bi-Week				x 26 Periods	
Month				x 12 Months	
Bi-Month				x 6 Periods	
Quarter				x 4 Quarters	
½ Year				x 2 Periods	
Annual				x 1 Period	

Total Annual Man Hour Requirements

Average Annual Hours/Full Time Employee

Number of Housekeeping Personnel

Reprinted with permission from "Housekeeping Manual for Retail Stores," NRMA, 1963; p40.

EXHIBIT 26

in any of these areas, such as emptying ash trays, an allowance is made for them. This is usually 10 per cent of the number of man-hours allotted to the major cleaning.

With the inventories and the man-hour figures before him, the housekeeping head can calculate how many man-hours are required, point by point, and come up with an annual total. To this figure, he adds an allowance for utility services the housekeeping staff will be expected to perform—trash removal, moving and porter services when departments expand or contract, cleaning of storage areas, and so on.

The grand total will be worked up in terms of man-hours. From this, the planner develops the number of people needed, and their payroll budget. If the budget is too high, priorities and frequencies can be re-examined, so that the cleaning is cut back where least harm is done.

Now, knowing what is to be done and how many hands will be available to him, he can work out daily, weekly, and monthly schedules and assign the tasks.

Organizing the Crew

The NRMA "Housekeeping Manual" recommends a corps of working supervisors, well trained and properly paid—preferably one for each housekeeping job. Each supervisor would lead a small team of two or three other housekeeping employees.

The manual recommends also that there be two or three levels of working supervisors, according to the size of the store. Among other reasons, such a set-up puts a ladder of advancement before the porters and maids and gives them something many of them now lack—an incentive to do a good job.

Full-time employees are preferable to part-timers for housekeeping work, and store-open hours, supplemented by early morning and early evening hours, are preferable to night shifts. Supervision is easier, utility costs are conserved, and the hazard of theft is lessened.

Day housekeeping employees should come in at six or seven in the morning, attack the heavy-traffic areas before customers appear on the scene, and busy themselves with light-traffic and backstage areas and periodic tidying up after the store opens. Heavy-duty cleaners and those performing utility services or answering emergency needs should be on the day shift. The late shift should come on at three or four in the afternoon and continue until after store closing—and its number should be kept small. One of their responsibilities should be to prepare and set out equipment and supplies for the day shift.

In any shift, however, there need be no worker struggling alone and ineffectually with a poorly organized job. When there is a working supervisor, each chore is tackled by a team and is handled with the tools and by the method specified for it.

Training and Re-Training

It is not easy to retrain people. The writers of the NRMA "Housekeeping Manual" warn against attempting a rapid transition from the casual methods that prevail in the typical store to the standardized operation that is needed. They suggest making haste slowly.

When the executive in charge of housekeeping has worked out his program in detail, including standards, procedures, frequencies, and budget, and has received approval for it, his next step is to select a very few outstanding housekeeping employees. These people he now trains as his first-rank working supervisors.

After the first group has learned what is expected of it, another group of above-average housekeeping employees is selected, to work with and be trained by the first few. And so on, until, little by little, he has his full complement of working supervisors.

Smaller Branches

The small branch with tiny housekeeping staff cannot readily set up an elaborate organization of its people. It can, however, apply the principles outlined here: inventorying the work to be done, establishing priorities, setting standards and procedures, estimating man-hours, and so on.

Careful selection of equipment, methods, and supplies is as important in the small unit as in the large ones. The smaller the staff, the less one can afford to waste precious hours of time with inefficient tools and methods.

If there are jobs that the small branch cannot handle efficiently, because the volume of work does not justify the purchase of proper equipment, the answer may lie in the use of outside services. Even when an outsider is used, however, the need for testing and reviewing remains.

Before a contract comes up for renewal, the branch manager should question his housekeeping head about any changes that may have developed during the life of the contract. These would include not only changes in the nature and amount of work to be done, but also the possibility that new equipment may have become available and may have reduced the need for contracting the work.

Reciprocal Responsibilities

The housekeeping staff has a responsibility to the branch's employees to give them a clean, tidy place to work—one that will encourage them to try to keep it as clean and tidy as they find it each day.

At the same time, the attitudes of the store staff should be such that the housekeeping employees are stimulated to do their best. Salespeople should keep their counters and other working areas neat, and should do whatever superficial cleaning is necessary to keep their departments bright and shining.

Office workers, including executives, should keep their own desks and file cabinet tops in order. Cleaners who have to move mounds of papers before they can dust desk tops are likely to skip the whole thing—or to spend entirely too much time on a simple task.

Receiving and marking employees, alteration people, and other behind-the-scenes workers should also be reminded to keep their work places tidy, so that there is no unnecessary load imposed on the housekeeping force—and so that the cleaners do not develop the feeling that the condition of these areas is a matter of indifference to all concerned.

Attitude and cooperation are, of course, very much the branch manager's province. Precept, example, and encouragement—even to the smile of approval when a salesperson picks up a scrap of paper from an aisle—are his tools. He can use them to get a cleaner store.

CHAPTER 22

CHECKS AND CONTROLS FOR
THE BRANCH MANAGER

To keep his finger on the pulse of his unit's operation, the branch manager needs a series of checks and controls. In this chapter is presented a list of some of the most needed of such controls. Not all are required at every branch, and some branches may need others as well. These, however, are fairly basic to most branches.

In order to use checks and controls effectively, quantitative and qualitative standards should first be set, so that there is a yardstick against which to measure performance. Where standards cannot be set immediately, as in a new branch in its first months of operation, the accumulated reports will in time provide a basis for establishing standards. The more consistently the reports and checks are used, the more useful they will be. And the more regularly the branch manager reviews them (and lets it be known that he does), the more conscientious his various supervisors will be in judging their own performance and seeking paths to improvement.

Personnel and Training Functions

1. Periodic (probably weekly) open-to-hire report by job description and department, including a comparison to last week and last year, and also including an aging of the unfilled openings.

2. Periodic (probably monthly) report on turnover by depart-

ment, division, and store, including comparison with most recent six months and last year.

3. Shopping services, to be sure training and orientation have accomplished their mission.

4. Monthly cumulative compensation, unemployment and liability reports, including a comparison to last year, to pinpoint unfavorable trends.

5. Accident report summary (monthly) by department, as check on effectiveness of safety program.

6. Monthly infirmary reports, limited to repeat visits above a specified number, to highlight problem employees.

7. Monthly reports of ratio of part time to full time employees.

8. Training program progress and status reports, to reflect activities of training department.

9. Employee facility inspection reports by personnel staff.

Selling Function

1. Graph of transactions, hour by hour, with superimposed graph of salesclerks on hand. Transactions might be tracked by hourly readings of registers.

2. Daily "book" by department, for comparison with clerk hours used.

3. Weekly reports of individual clerk average "books."

4. Weekly error control reports, cash register error and shortage reports, missing sales check reports, as indications of salesclerk efficiency.

Receiving and Marking

1. Aging report (twice a week or more often) listing every shipment still in marking room beyond specified standard (24 hours, 48 hours, or any other). Include receiving number, date of receipt, resource, number of units, department, reason for delay.

2. Production reports (weekly) of total productivity in units processed per work hour, compared to last year and to preceding weeks.

3. Carryover report: Running daily report of shipments carried

over, shipments received, shipments processed, shipments left at end of day.

Order Checking

If orders are placed by branch:
1. Aging reports.
2. Productivity reports.
3. Carryover reports.

Transfers

1. Outgoing carryovers, if any—really an exception report in most branches.
2. Incoming carryovers of goods not delivered to floor—an exception report in most branches.
3. Transfer requests, if centrally initiated, might be channeled through a central source for recording and subsequent check-off when shipments leave the building. A simple report of unprocessed transfers once or twice a week is usually adequate.

Stockkeeping

This is an area in which in-person observation is most desirable. However, a simple check list should be filled out by floor or division managers and submitted on a prescheduled basis reporting: general orderliness and logical arrangement; status of pending markdowns; damage accumulations; status of refunds awaiting examination and return to stock; new receipts waiting to be put away, pending vendor returns; pending transfers; protection of merchandise; cleanliness; evidence of smoking; segregation of advertised goods; condition of customer "Holds," etc.

Markdowns and Reticketing

1. Receiving Department should provide aging, carryover, and production reports, as for new goods.
2. Selling Department delays can be flagged by reporting re-

ceipt of documents over one day old (or whatever time lag store considers permissible).

3. For price changes initiated centrally, controls similar to those described for transfers can be employed.

Vendor Returns and Repairs

1. Receiving and marking department should provide aging, carryover, and production reports, as for markdowns.

2. Departmental efficiency can be checked by reports of receipt of all documents over one day (or other period) old.

3. For centrally initiated vendor-return requests, controls similar to those described for transfers can be employed.

Wrapping, Packing, and Delivery

1. If handled in-store, carryover and productivity reports can fulfill the need.

2. If handled from the main store, use:

   a. Spot checks by calling customers to confirm delivery and any time lag.
   b. Review and appraisal of non-delivery complaints.

3. For mail and phone orders, taken centrally, analysis of complaint statistics can be used as a means of checking.

Furniture, Rugs, Appliances

The negative barometer of complaint activity and cancellations is a check on delivery and service. Spot-check procedure is possible by following up specific transactions.

Maintenance and Housekeeping

1. Monthly expense statements, with comparisons to last year.

2. Report of actual accomplishments as compared to predetermined preventive maintenance requirements.

3. Housekeeping service checks against list of items (as discussed at length in chapter on this subject.) Personal observation and awareness are most important.

4. Report of actual work performed as compared with programmed schedule of housekeeping assignments.

Adjustments

1. If handled locally, then regular aging, carryover, and productivity reports provide control.

2. Wherever handled, the frequency and nature of second complaints should be recorded, tabulated, reported, and studied.

Workrooms

1. Aging, carryover, and productivity reports measure performance.

2. Customer surveys and service shoppings provide additional checks.

Fitting Rooms

1. Periodic inspections against previously drawn checklist, similar to those suggested for housekeeping (in chapter on that subject.)

Telephone Service

1. Regular tests of waiting time on incoming calls.
2. Service and courtesy checks.

APPENDIX A

THE TOP MANAGEMENT SURVEY

Heads of branch-owning NRMA member stores cooperated in the preparation of this book by responding to a five-page questionnaire, circulated among them by mail, in order to obtain their point of view on the branch, the branch manager, and his job.

Findings of that survey appear in tabloid form below:

Volume, Main and All Branch or Sister Stores Combined:

19%—under $10 million
48 —$10 to $50 million
33 —over $50 million

100%

Number of Branches:

13%—one branch
19 —two branches
12 —three
12 —four
9 —five
35 —six or more

100%

Number of Branches To Be Opened by End of Following Year:

18%—none
25 —one
7 —two
10 —three or more
40 —no answer

100%

Special Types of Branches:

  86% have one or more in a suburban shopping center
  45% have one or more branches on a city street
  43% have one or more doing less than $2 million a year
  31% have one or more less than five miles from the main store
  30% have one or more further than 50 miles from the main store
  26% have one or more "twigs"
  24% have one or more free standing branches
  13% have one or more doing over $20 million a year

Services Performed Centrally for Any or All of the Stores Branches:

  98% prepare ads
  94% authorize credit
  94% purchase supplies
  92% do sales audit
  88% receive and mark
  86% do payroll
  82% plan displays
  82% keep reserve stocks
  21% hire rank-and-file employees
  21% train rank-and-file employees

Steps Taken by Branches to Encourage Good Community Relations:

  93% Manager is personally active in community affairs
  81% Branch participates in local drives, celebrations, etc.
  45% Youth activities, teen clubs, etc.
  31% Branch makes meeting rooms available to local clubs

Other: Service clubs, fashion shows, membership in business and civic associations, charm course, employment of DE students, cooperation in Business-Industry Education Day.

Individual Comments: "Activity in general community efforts rather than neighborhood efforts." "All branches in metropolitan area, so most of our participation is on corporate basis." "We work hard to have our stores accepted as local institutions." "We have consumer advisory board of local club women at each store." "Mostly through merchants association."

Branches That Encountered a Problem Winning Acceptance:

5% have experienced problems

Individual Comments: "Managers take positions of leadership in shopping center association." "We hire local people, use local newspapers." "Always sympathetic and helpful as we can be on local matters."

Executive to Whom Branch Managers Report:

  62%—President, general manager, etc.
  18 —Vice-president in charge of branch stores
   9 —District manager (usually chain-type organizations)
   6 —General merchandise manager
   4 —Sales promotion manager
   1 —Operations manager
 100%

Number of Times Typical Buyer Visits Each Branch:

  15%—one to nine times a year
  32 —ten to 19
  29 —20 to 29
   4 —30 to 39
  20 —40 or more
 100%
Median: 21-22 times a year

Executives, Other Than Buyers, Who Visit Branches Regularly:

69%—Merchandise manager, divisional merchandise managers
33%—President, other top management
31%—Operations manager
22%—Controller, treasurer
19%—Personnel manager
19%—Display manager
12%—Sales promotion, advertising manager
18%—All
 3%—None

Other: General merchandising vice-presidents have representatives in the branches to coordinate merchandising activities.

Regularly Scheduled Meetings for Branch Executives:

78% have branch executives meet at the main store with their opposite numbers

58%—have meetings with opposite numbers at other branches

Individual Comment: "Periodically meet with executives with same job responsibility in other stores in group meetings held in parent store building." "Each manager attends weekly executive meetings at parent store." "We started with group meetings. Now we break down into meetings of merchandising and operating personnel separately." "Branch executives visit main store weekly." "Sales promotion has monthly meeting for all branches." "Communication is by phone. Managers visit each other." "Buyers have quarterly meetings with department managers and store managers. Vice-president in charge of stores has monthly meetings for branch managers. Managers come to monthly executive meetings." "Merchandise meeting monthly, combining promotional and local information." "Branch manager attends weekly advertising meeting." "Branch store managers attend all merchandise and fashion meetings at main store." "Sales supervisors visit downtown on weekly basis." "All managers and supervisors attend joint meeting with managers and supervisors of all stores at least once a month." "Quarterly meetings attended by all branch store managers, store president, chairman of board, general merchandise manager, sales promotion head, general superintendent. Store president conducts the sessions. Subjects are problems previouly submitted by branch managers for these meetings. They last about half a day and are very productive." "Rotating branch meetings." "Line presentations." "Monthly meetings for top groups, more frequently at lower lewels." "Meetings several times yearly in centrally located hotel." "Monthly luncheon meetings." "Branch managers invited to all operating and merchandising meetings, and are thus kept current on all problems." "Branch managers meet at main store about once a month. Jawbone with proper person about specific problem areas."

Merchandising Authority Given to Branch:

85%—may request items not planned for them
70%—consulted on sales and stock goals
52%—do routine reordering of basics
34%—may reorder hot sellers
34%—may reject merchandise they don't want
29%—may mark down slow items
12%—none at all
 7%—complete; they do own buying

Individual Comment: "Very little authority but do criticize assortments and are listened to." "Authority granted depends upon branch department manager's experience and judgment." "Branch originates markdowns only on soiled, damaged, lost goods." "Buyer is encouraged to delegate merchandising authority to local department manager as to ordering basics, reordering hot items, etc." "Branches work with buyers in setting seasonal model stock levels. Then branches are held responsible for staying in stock accordingly. Comparison shopping function is coordinator and sometimes policeman."

Steps Most Effective in Keeping Branches Properly Stocked:

73%—analyze sales and stock reports
57%—check unit controls
52%—management inspects personally
46%—analyze requisitions and want slips
43%—shop branch stocks
42%—leave it to buyers
25%—keep separate open-to-buy for branches
16%—require merchandise diaries from branches

Individual Comment: "Frequent visits to branch by the buyers." "Keep separate stock figures for branches in a sizeable portion. Automatic reordering of basics." "Basic stock audit program very effective." "Weekly list of needs." "We are on computer and also use basic stock for staples." "Have to depend on buyers to large degree."

Procedure on Branch Requests for Merchandise:

58% require written requisitions.

Of those who do:
57% send copies routinely to branch manager
65% send copies also to an executive of main store

Individual Comment: "Unit control books act as requisition. Channel through branch manager, parent divisional merchandise manager and general merchandise manager. Compliance with fill-ins is measured by independent merchandise information office and reported to management." "Direct phone to parent store expedites request." "We have pretty extensive pool stocks of basics. These require requisitions. Other requests can be treated informally." "Our requisitions are documents which authorize shipments." "Not formalized, but must live up to planned assortments." "Make much use of phone requests. If not quickly filled, written request is made, with copies to divisional and general merchandise managers." "Buyers who are good buyers have important commitment to branch needs."

Buyer Understanding of Branch Needs:

80% say most buyers understand branch needs adequately

Individual Comment: "Most buyers still never accept fact that stock should be distributed to stores in relation to sales. They tend to overstock the downtown store."

Branch Experience as Part of Buyer's Training:

14% require this

Individual Comment: "Our chain of promotion involves branch service." "Junior executive invariably gets branch experience. Improbable that a person without branch experience would be promoted to buyer. Could be hired from outside."

Extent to Which Main Store Advertising Covers Branch Needs:

62%—Branches need some additional local media
49%—Main store advertising does the entire job
16%—Branch advertising often differs in content and character
8%—Each branch prepares and places own advertising

Individual Comment: "In our metropolitan area, there is no problem, but out-of-town stores' advertising has to be tailored to their needs." "We run complete ad schedule for each branch store, in addition to whatever they get out of the main store ads. We do all advertising at the main store." "Branches participate with their respective shopping center organizations." "Our branches participate in all store-wide promotions. In addition, they need a certain amount of individual promotion, as in shopping center promotions. Twice a year we run branch store sales for which merchandising responsibility and authority rest with the branch store manager. These are extremely productive." "We use basic list of papers which have statewide distribution, plus local papers." "Branches are included in all downtown ads plus separate ads in local papers and shopping center tabloids." "Branch is in city 40 miles distant. Its advertising is done in that city's papers and radio only." "All stores well covered by metropolitan city's newspaper. We also use radio and TV."

Steps Taken To See That Branches Are Prepared for
"Also At Branches" Advertising:

92%—Branches get monthly schedules of upcoming ads and events
53%—Buyer must notify branch of specific ads—usually 10 days ahead
43%—Advertising department must notify branch—usually 7 days ahead
20%—Branches help plan and schedule such ads and events
17%—Management requires report of branch results on such ads

Individual Comment: "When shopping center events dictate, branches help plan and schedule ads." "Central advertising department issues ad proofs to buyer for correction and local paper sends 'information only' proof to branch manager of store concerned about three days before ad runs." "Each department manager receives ad requisition in advance of running." "Buyers and merchandisers are responsible for ad coverage at branches." "Branch manager attends advance planning of advertising. Monthly meeting between buyers and sales managers keeps everyone informed." "Branch receives extra copy of store department's ad copy requisition." "When ad copy is written, a duplicate is sent to branch store manager." "Our advertising copy form indicates if merchandise is available at the branches."

Attitude Toward Increased Branch Responsibility for
Advertising and Promotion:

90% say branches should not take more responsibility

Individual Comment: "Branch managers are too busy as it is." "Too apt to be locally influenced. Would dilute our budget." "Program must be centrally coordinated." "No, because of buying centrally. Believe it is a corporate responsibility." "Area is too compact for uncentralized and diverse efforts." "More responsibility. Branches are aware of what is needed in their areas." "More responsibility would bring increased sales and reduced markdowns." "Store manager must have control of advertising and promotion that affect his branch only."

Branch Inventory Figures:

    50% keep all inventories separately for each branch
     5   keep some separately
    45 have no separate inventories
   100%

Branch Operating Statements:

    80% carry branch operating statements through to contribution
    87% carry branch operating statements through to net operating profit or loss

Charges for Centrally Performed Services:

    79% make such charges to the branch
    The usual basis is proration according to volume.

Factors Other Than Financial Considered in Judging Branch Operation:

    64% consider such factors

    Factors Named: Growth. Customer service. Share of local market. Volume. Image. Socio-economic. Position in community. Staple checks. Housekeeping. New ideas. Number of promotions to buyer. Corporate citizenship. Physical appearance. Future potential.

Branch Manager's Responsibilities:

    50% have written job description for branch manager
    23% have written job description for assistant branch manager

Most Important Elements of Branch Manager's Job:

    In order of frequency: Merchandising, personnel, volume, customer service, leadership, making a profit, administration, expense control, liaison with main store, no one element.

Most Important Subjects to Cover in Manual for Branch Managers:

    In order of frequency: Merchandising, personnel and leadership, liaison with main store, shortage and expense control, operations, community relations, promotion, administration, display, customer service.

Subjects Needing Coverage at Branch Managers' Seminars:

In order of frequency: Merchandising, liaison and communications, shortage and expense control, leadership, operations, community relations, customer service, promotions, profit making.

The Branch of the Future:

68% expect it to be larger

81% expect it to be more independent of the parent

97% expect it to make a greater contribution to volume and profit.

Individual Comment: "Branches of the future should be large enough to convey the image of the parent store and satisfy most of the needs of the communities they are to serve." "If branches are beyond a 20-mile radius of the downtown store, they will have to be less dependent upon it. A branch 200 miles distant might receive and deliver its own merchandise, and have its own buying and advertising staff." "In the larger cities, the trend is to larger branches, but there is still a need for smaller branches at convenient locations to serve certain locales." "With multi-unit set-up, we expect less independence." "Trend is toward main buying office set-up." "More self-sufficient to cope with specific competitive factors affecting branch location." "Buying will become more centralized, but merchandising responsibility will be more de-centralized." "A branch operation is necessary for total store profit."

APPENDIX B

THE BRANCH MANAGERS' SURVEY

Among the ways in which branch managers themselves cooperated in the preparation of this book was to respond to a five-page questionnaire, circulated among them by mail. Through this medium, they expressed their viewpoint on their jobs, and on what they need to meet their responsibilities successfully.

Findings of that survey appear in tabloid form below:

Total Annual Sales of Branch Operated:

    15 %—under $1 million
    25   —$1 to $3 million
    12½ —$3 to $5 million
    25   —$5 to $10 million
    22½ —over $10 million
    ─────
    100 %
    Median, $5 million

Size of Branch in Relation to Parent:

    25%—10% of less of total from all units
    25 —11% to 20% of total from all units
    50 —more than 20% of total from all units
    ─────
    100%
    Median, 20% of total

Square Footage of Branch:

    37%—under 50,000 sq. ft.
    22 —50,000 to 99,999 sq. ft.
    20 —100,000 to 149,000 sq. ft.
    21 —over 150,000 sq. ft.
    ─────
    100%
    Median, 75,000 sq. ft.

Location of Branch:

    45%—shopping center
    28 —remote, in city other than parent store's city
    17 —suburban
    <u>10 —city</u>
    100%

Degree of Autonomy:

    68%—non-autonomous; major policies and control set by parent
    15 —autonomous, with full authority vested in manager
    <u>17 —semi-autonomous; other variations</u>
    100%

Facilities at Branch for Handling All or Nearly All of Its Work:

    91%—employment
    88%—training
    37%—receiving
    37%—marking
    27%—credit
    22%—unit controls
    15%—advertising
    15%—sales audit
    3%—none of these functions

Other Phases of Operation Handled Largely at Branch:

    50%—none
    24%—display
    15%—merchandising
    13%—alterations
    8%—public relations
    5%—fashion shows
    5%—delivery

Preference as to Degree of Decentralization of Facilities:

    57%—prefer more decentralization
    30 —would want no change
    <u>13 —prefer less decentralization</u>
    100%

Activities Managers Prefer to Decentralize:

In order of freqeuncy: Merchandising generally; reordering of basics; receiving and marking; advertising; display.

Individual Comment: "Would like to see complete authority for writing reorders, based on realistic rate of sale. Agree that initial orders should be placed centrally. Would like to be able to initiate markdowns on slow-selling merchandise." "It is my opinion that some phases of merchandising the branch are better understood by the branch manager than by the merchandising division." "We should be able to reorder basics to maintain stock position, have a larger share of markdown budgets, run unit stock control, order direct from suppliers for all basics, and have more say in advertising programs." "We feel that buying and merchandising should be handled centrally, with manager of suburban store given responsibility to run the store." "Receiving and marking at branch would speed up flow of basic fill-ins, which are so important in a branch." "Direct purchase of display props." "More participation in advertising and conference on merchandise to be handled, especially basic stocks." "Credit, for faster processing. Too much time elapses from time application is taken until credit is granted or refused." "Local advertising." "Buying function."

Branch Manager's Most Important Responsibility:

55%—personnel
53%—merchandising
23%—sales
10%—profit
10%—display

Others: Customer service, public relations, expense control, maintenance, liaison with main store.

Individual Comment: "To keep smooth flow of merchandise into the branch and to hire and train and keep a good staff of selling people." "To maintain a stock position which meets the demands of our immediate trade area." "Presentation of merchandise in proper manner." "Analysis of sales to plan merchandise needs." "Community relations." "Assume leadership in shopping center merchants association." "Train and develop executive and sales personnel." "Department location and fixturing and space." "Supervision, training, and guidance of department managers and other supervisors." "To maintain troop morale."

"Control of all expense centers within the store." "Developing a spirit of cooperation, communication and coordination between personnel of branch and the mother store." "Organization, leadership, development of sales personnel." "Training department managers to become buyers." "To serve and sell." "Managing people." "Customer service." "Would like to be able to say merchandise control."

Division of Responsibility Between Manager and Assistant:

Primarily manager's responsibility:

    93%—community relations
    93%—liaison with parent store
    91%—planning future growth
    87%—merchandising
    83%—promotion
    76%—analysis of competition

Primarily assistant's responsibility:

    82%—customer service
    71%—systems, accounting
    65%—store operation *
    60%—personnel management *

Individual Comments: "I believe the manager should assume responsibility in all major functions of the store and assign the specific duties within each function." "Manager and assistant share the work." "Both should work in close harmony in all problems that pertain to the business." "Depends on individual background." "Satisfied. Assistant handles store operation, systems, personnel. Manager, the rest." "I believe manager's responsibility should be primarily merchandising. System of checks and balances for other functions." "We are now adding an operations assistant manager in addition to two merchandise assistants. This will enable the store manager to take a greater share in merchandise planning." "We have no hard and fast responsibilities. We work very closely on many functions." "Depends on background and needs of branch." "I would like another assistant to share the merchandising responsibility."

* Many of the reporting branch managers consider this a shared responsibility, not clearly assignable to either one alone.

Background That Branch Manager Brought to Job:
- 85%—merchandising
- 15%—operations
- 15%—previously owned or managed a store
- 10%—sales
- *Other:* Sales promotion, display, control, research.

Background That Assistant Manager Brought to Job:
- 50%—merchandising
- 40%—operations
- 15%—sales
- 12%—store manager
- 10%—personnel
- *Other:* display, accounting, credit.

Background Preferred for Future Branch Managers:
- 95%—merchandising
- 26%—operations
- 13%—personnel

Other: Management, credit, public relations, promotion, display, all phases, branch operation, accounting, varied, doesn't matter, from ranks.

Background Preferred for Future Branch Assistant Managers:
- 66%—merchandising
- 45%—operations
- 21%—personnel
- 12%—accounting, control

Other: Promotion, customer service, sales, display, credit, what manager lacks, willingness, from ranks.

Most Needed Subjects in Manual for Branch Executives:
- 65%—personnel and training
- 62%—merchandising
- 24%—expense control
- 18%—promotion and advertising
- 18%—security
- 18%—liaison, communications
- 15%—organization, policies
- 12%—layout, fixturing

Others: Salesmanship, classification merchandising, housekeeping, display, operations, simplification of paper work, shopping center relations, operating statistics, management of own time.

Subjects Considered Especially Vital in Book on Branch Management:

In order of frequency: Expense control, shortage control, personnel management, merchandise control methods, salesmanship, store housekeeping, training techniques, display techniques, promotional planning, merchandise budgeting, layout and fixturing, receiving and marking, using classification data, materials handling, parking problems, technique of fashion shows, merchandising arithmetic, credit management, using EDP.

Individual Comments: "A manager should be more or less knowledgeable in all areas." "Executive development and motivation." "Ways to improve communications between mother store and branch." "Branch management, especially in stores remote from parent, needs general coverage." "Something like the Buyer's Manual." "Increasing sales productivity." "How to work with a shopping center association and how to set up a promotional budget for shopping centers, and the best method to assure participation by all stores." "Handling of employees." "Procedure for handling shoplifters." "Executive development and motivation." "Understanding human behavior." "How to keep on top of items." "The whys and wherefores of personnel management." "Basic stock control." "Methods to increase volume at department level." "Techniques of expense control." "The importance of being a merchant." "The need for training young, eager personnel." "Simplification of paper work." "Promotional planning." "Getting and training better salespeople." "Inventory control by classifications." "Having a balanced approach to the job. It is too easy to devote more time than is advisable to one particular element while others suffer." "Techniques of supervision." "Basic stock systems, including direct ordering from vendors." "Proper movement of merchandise between parent department and all branch store departments." "Liaison." "Operating statistics." "Stock fill-in programs."

APPENDIX C

BRANCH STORE ORGANIZATION AND JOB DESCRIPTIONS

One of the most complete descriptions of branch store organization is that developed by Hutzler's of Baltimore, to guide its suburban stores and the executives at the main store who are responsible for working with them.

With the graciously given permission of the store, the entire plan of organization is reproduced here. Note that each branch store executive's responsibilities are spelled out in detail, from manager down to sponsor. Following this material, the line and staff responsibilities of the downtown store's executives for branch functions are also spelled out.

HUTZLER'S SUBURBAN STORES ORGANIZATION

Hutzler's Suburban Stores Organization will be primarily a selling group backed by the specialized merchandising and operating organization of the Downtown Store. The success of the Suburban Store is dependent on the ability of the Suburban Stores to use the facilities and services of the Downtown Store.

Plan of Operation

Within the framework of Hutzler policy, the Suburban Stores Management has the authority and responsibility to make the day to day operating decisions.

The Manager and the Assistant Manager of each Suburban Store will act as senior and junior partners of a business. They must know of each other's duties and plans and act in each other's place when one or the other is absent. Close teamwork is essential in the operation.

251

Responsibilities of the Suburban Store Executives

General Suburban Stores Manager

1. To report to the General Manager.
2. To maintain the reputation, efficiency, progress and profit of the Suburban Stores.
3. To consult with the Downtown Store "general managers" in order constantly to improve the Suburban Stores' performance.
4. To determine standards in joint conference with the Downtown Store "general managers."

Manager

1. To report to the General Suburban Stores Manager.
2. To direct and coordinate the proper merchandising and other operations of the Suburban Store.
3. To consult with the Downtown Store Managers in order constantly to improve the operations and merchandising of the Suburban Stores which include the maintenance of stocks in proper quantities and assortments.
4. To maintain the most effective display of merchandise.

Assistant Manager

1. To report to the Manager.
2. To provide a service of information, advice, and assistance to the customers and employees of the Suburban Store so that the maximum selling effectiveness of the store will be realized.
3. To provide the best selling techniques which will result in high productivity and low costs.

Specific responsibilities will include:

The employment of personnel, the handling of personnel records and the over-all personnel administration.
The system and primary selling training.
The maintenance or proper store service.
The operation of the Medical Department.
The operation of the Protection Department.

The Office, Personnel and Training functions may be grouped under one supervisor or divided into two supervisory assignments depending on the needs of the individual Suburban Store. This applies also to the Operating and Selling functions.

The same situation may exist in the operating and maintenance supervisory functions.

Office Supervisor

1. To report to the Assistant Manager.
2. To supervise the clerical functions and to handle other duties that may be delegated by the Assistant Manager.

   Specific responsibilities will include:

   Adjustments
   Cashiering
   Clerical Functions
   Credit Office
   C.O.D. Will Calls
   Correspondence
   Office Supplies
   Repair Services
   Pay Office
   Telephone Switchboard
   Personnel Records
   Interviewing Applicants
   Employing Personnel

Personnel and Training Supervisor

1. To report to the Assistant Manager.
2. To supervise the personnel and training functions and to handle other duties that may be delegated by the Assistant Manager.

   Specific responsibilities will include:

   Interviewing applicants.
   Employing personnel.
   Necessary routines and follow up in connection with personnel problems.
   Conducting training classes.
   Follow up on employee system errors.
   Shopping report system.
   To be prepared to substitute for the Selling Supervisor.

Selling Supervisor

1. To report to the Assistant Manager.
2. To maintain Hutzler selling service standards through constant supervision of the selling service and by taking prompt action to resolve any selling coverage problems.

Specific responsibilities will include:

To regularly consult with the Sales Supervisors so as to be aware of their coverage problems.

To promptly suggest to the Assistant Manager any changes, either increases or decreases, in basic or contingent force that current conditions create as to scheduling and service.

To review daily the opening and closing supervisory schedules and make substitutions where required.

To supervise the selling squad, making their daily assignments, and see that the squad personnel are constantly being trained to sell in all departments.

To check absenteeism on store opening and make the necessary adjustments.

To anticipate vacation replacement needs by section and to make specific squad replacements as early as possible for the following week.

Operating Supervisor

1. To report to the Assistant Manager.
2. To supervise the operating functions of the store and to handle other duties that may be delegated by the Assistant Manager.

Specific responsibilities will include:

Floor and central wrapping
Housekeeping
Alteration and Busheling
Watchmen
Stockkeeping
Wrapping supplies
Take-with wrapping desks
Merchandising Handling
Floor cashiers
Window cleaning

Maintenance Supervisor

1. To report to the Assistant Manager.
2. To supervise the functions of maintenance, repair and upkeep of the building and equipment and to handle other duties that may be delegated by the Assistant Manager.

   Specific responsibilities will include:
   Heating, air conditioning
   Lighting
   Plumbing
   Electrical
   Painting
   Carpentry
   Escalators, elevators and other equipment

Food Supervisor(s)

1. To report to the Assistant Manager.
2. To supervise the operation of the food departments, including workroom functions and service to customers and employees.

   a. Specific merchandise responsibilities will include:
      1. Obtaining from the Manager of Food Departments menus of restaurant foods and catering foods, and assortments for bakery production that are suitable for the Suburban Store.
      2. The preparation of food served in the customer and employee restaurants.
      3. Keeping the Manager of Food Departments informed of the acceptance by the Suburban Store customers of the assortments offered.
      4. Consulting with the Suburban Store Assistant Manager in order to constantly improve the selections offered and to increase sales.

   b. Specific service responsibilities will include:
      1. Planning of selling and production forces, scheduling of hours, days off and vacations—within limits provided by the Suburban Store Management.
      2. Follow up training of all personnel within their group area.
      3. Selling Service.

  4. Adjustments.
  5. Wrapping and cashiering service.
  6. Appearance of department.
  7. Closing of departments at end of day.

 c. Specific workroom responsibilities will include:

  1. Requisitioning and/or purchasing of ingredients and supplies; and maintenance and forwarding of records and documents as directed by the Manager of Food Departments.
  2. Preparation of foods and manufacture of bakery products according to *Hutzler standards of quality, appearance and sanitation,* as directed by the Manager of Food Departments.
  3. Informing the Manager of Food Departments of deficiencies or overstocks of ingredients and supplies.
  4. Security of food inventories.
  5. Waste control.

Display Supervisor

1. To report to the Manager.
2. To see that the store decorating meets the Hutzler standard.
3. To supervise Display personnel.

Sales Supervisors

1. To report to the Manager for merchandising operations and to Assistant Manager for service functions.
2. To supervise all activities within their group areas.

 a. Merchandise responsibilities will include:

  1. Obtaining merchandise suitable for the Suburban Store from the buyers of the departments in their group.
  2. Informing the buyers of any deficiencies in stock.
  3. Consulting with the Manager in order constantly to improve the selection of merchandise in the store.
  4. Seeing that slow moving merchandise is promptly returned to the Downtown Store.

 b. Service responsibilities will include:

  1. Planning of the sales force, scheduling of individual hours, days off, and vacations—within limits provided by Management.

2. Merchandise and follow-up selling training of salespeople.
3. Selling service.
4. Floor adjustments and returns.
5. Wrapping service.
6. Appearance of department.
7. Closing of department at end of day.

Detailed Responsibilities of the Sales Supervisor

A. *Requisitioning Merchandise*

1. To see that stock is kept complete in price lines, styles, sizes, colors, and materials in those lines which have been established as running numbers in the department. Requisitions should be timed in order to insure delivery of the merchandise when needed.
2. Review sales on the items checked after each count period.
3. Keeping the Manager and Buyer informed at all times as to wanted and unwanted merchandise.
4. Prepare merchandise requisitions to replenish model stocks and to replenish other stocks in order to meet unusual needs.

B. *Securing New Merchandise*

To help the Buyer at all times in planning for new merchandise, following up the demand through the salespeople, sponsors, calls, special orders, stock lists, and other records.

C. *Following Up Requisitioned Merchandise*

1. To keep informed about the status of all unfilled merchandise requisitions and be sure that everything is being done to expedite the replenishment of stock.
2. Never hesitate to telephone for merchandise which is needed.
3. If difficulty is encountered in obtaining replenishment of fast selling items or other merchandise, to promptly inform the Manager.

D. *Receiving Merchandise*

1. To make checks of incoming merchandise for correct price tickets and completeness of the stock received according to requisitions.

2. To check the condition of merchandise received.
3. To keep merchandise for their group coming through without unnecessary delay.

E. *Maintenance of Stock*

1. Through constant use of the sales records, stock lists, and stock analysis, to have the stock which is needed.
2. To be constantly aware each day of the best sellers in the group and to keep Manager and Buyer promptly informed.
3. To keep the Manager and the Buyers informed of significant sales trends and item developments.
4. To follow through on want slips procedure.
5. Thoroughly understand all seasonal merchandise and timing problems as they apply to departments in the group.
6. The proper timing of seasonal peak stocks in terms of seasonal sales variation.
7. Responsible for developing each department of the group to its greatest merchandise effectiveness through constant item planning.
8. Proper maintenance of the stock systems.
9. Recommends stock depth changes, item changes, mark-downs, items for advertising promotion, and other merchandising actions to Manager and Buyer.
10. Inventories over-age merchandise as requested.

F. *Information about the Merchandise*

1. To give the sponsors and salespeople all the information possible about merchandise, styles, seasons' trend, and the like to help them in their selling.
2. To supervise and instruct all new salespeople in:
   a. All phases of merchandise—location, types, styles, sizes, uses, colors, lines, handling, and care.
   b. Special practices in the group and system difficulties.
   c. Salesmanship—adapting general salesmanship principles to the group in specific detail.
   d. Articles in Trade Journals pertaining to the department.
3. To see that all people in the group know what is advertised and on display and the main features of each article.

4. Be sure salespeople know the salient selling points, media, location, of advertised merchandise and reserve stock.

5. Be sure salespeople are instructed that when they are unable to locate a wanted item, they are to check the stockroom, but not as a general practice to inform the customer that they will call the Downtown Store for information. If the salesperson is unable to find a wanted item and a satisfactory substitute cannot be found, the salesperson should refer the request to the Sponsor or the Sales Supervisor for assistance.

6. To hold weekly promotional and operational meetings with the salespeople to review and discuss plans and procedures.

7. To plan the selling force in the group and see that the Sponsors are properly trained for authorized signature responsibilities, for inspecting incoming merchandise for completeness of requisitions.

8. Keeping Sponsors fully informed as to statistical results of group sales and plans.

9. Through proper leadership by working with the Sponsors and salespeople to concentrate on slow selling merchandise so that markdowns may be avoided.

G. *Price Change of Merchandise in Stock*

1. To have all soiled or damaged merchandise taken out of stock and returned to the Downtown Store. When soiled or damaged merchandise is discovered and wanted by a customer, the Sales Supervisor has the authority to reduce the merchandise, being sure to make out the necessary Price Change Report.

2. To call to the attention of the Manager and the Buyer all slow selling merchandise that seems to need markdown.

3. To see that all necessary markdowns are carried through.

4. To see that all necessary markups are taken.

H. *Comparison of Merchandise*

1. To cooperate with the Comparison Office in every way by showing merchandise to shoppers and by asking that they shop competitors when necessary.

2. To keep the Manager and Buyer informed of merchandise in competing stores in the neighborhood through following up windows and their advertisements, and through shopping items of special interest or asking salespeople in group to do it.

I. *Newspaper Advertising*

1. To see that there is adequate stock in the department to cover this publicity.
2. To see that all people in the group know what is advertised and on display and the main features of each article.
3. To check advertised items to be certain all sizes, colors, and styles at the correct price are on hand the day the advertisement is run, and that the merchandise is correctly signed and displayed.
4. To help the Buyer in supplying ideas for advertisements.
5. To follow up these advertisements to see that they are absolutely accurate and satisfactory.
6. Maintain results of all advertisements pertaining to the group.

J. *Display of Merchandise*

1. To see that the group has on display any merchandise that is new, that is specially advertised, that is a special value.
2. To see that signs in the department are correct in every detail and that they are requisitioned in time for needs.
3. To know all merchandise from the group that is on display in own or in other groups.
4. To furnish ideas and merchandise, working with the display representative.
5. To help with any promotional projects, such as radio, fashion shows, etc.
6. To call to the attention of the Manager the need for changes in physical selling facilities and displays.

K. *Service*

1. Seeing that Hutzler service is constantly being given to customers and that the best selling standards are being maintained.
2. Answering customer inquiries and being alert to customer requests for little services.
3. Completing customer adjustments on selling floor and referring policy and questionable adjustments to the office.
4. Reporting any item needing repair or maintenance to the Operating and/or Maintenance Supervisor immediately.
5. Arranging for alterations and other Workroom services.

6. Seeing that each department is maintained in accordance with Hutzler standards, and that good housekeeping and good stock keeping is evident.
7. Closing departments at the end of store hours—completing flash reports, collecting salescheck envelopes, collecting tissue envelopes, ringing out registers.

L. *Personnel*

1. Frequent consultations with the Assistant Manager concerning personnel, customer service, and training.
2. Consultation with the Assistant Manager on department reviews.
3. Sales Supervisors will be rated on the satisfactory management of their group, based on the results attained, together with the opinion of the Buyer and the Suburban Store Management.

M. *Clerical Work*

To see that the clerical work of the department is done accurately and on time. This means the clerical routine incident to:
1. Dealing with parent departments—requisitions, special orders, returns, reports, etc.
2. Departmental records. Records of the sort required in that group—markdowns, markups, stock records, and the required daily, weekly, and monthly summaries.

Responsibilities of Sponsor

The Sponsor is responsible to the Supervisor and assumes such duties as delegated by the Supervisor.

In the absence of the Supervisor, the Sponsor shall substitute for the Supervisor.

General Responsibilities of All Supervisory Personnel

Supervision, in its broad sense, means having an efficient team to carry out the designated plan of operation and maintaining good morale.

Some of the major responsibilities include:

1. Planning the work of the people reporting to the executive.

2. Training the personnel and specifically training an understudy to assume the total responsibility of the executive in case of promotion, absence, or illness.
3. Keeping currently informed about things which will contribute to the efficiency of the operation.
4. Exercising the authority which is delegated.
5. Coordination of work with the work of other Supervisors.
6. Simplification, elimination, or consolidation of all activities which are not essential.
7. Coordination and supervision of all personnel; periodic rating.
8. Making any reports which are required by the Suburban Store Management of the Downtown Store Management.

Line and Staff Responsibilities of Downtown Manager's Division for Suburban Store Operation

Line Responsibilities

1. Assisting in unusual recruiting and training problems.
2. The purchasing and distribution of operating supplies.

Staff Responsibilities

1. A continuing review and analysis of the Suburban Store personnel and their performance of the functions for which the General Personnel and Service Manager's Division is responsible in the Downtown Store.
2. Recommending action to effect improvements.
3. Providing service, operating and personnel information, advice, and assistance.

Line and Staff Responsibilties of the Manager of Food Departments for Suburban Store Operation

Line Responsibilities

1. Sales Planning.
2. Menu Planning and Programming Bakery Production.
3. Centralized purchasing of ingredients (and such supplies as are his responsibility).
4. Designation and control of purchasing of ingredients which should be delegated to the Suburban Store Food Supervisors.

5. The prompt handling of requisitions out of the supply of centrally purchased ingredients.
6. Maintaining the Food Cost Accounting for each suburban store.
7. Continuing review of customer preference of selections offered in each suburban store.
8. Continuing inspection of restaurants, kitchens and bakeries for the purpose of directing Suburban Store Food Supervisors in maintaining Hutzler standards of quality, appearance, and sanitation.
9. The requisitioning of all signs needed for restaurant and bake shop promotion.

Staff Responsibilities

1. A continuing review and analysis of the Suburban Store Food Departments operations.
2. Recommending action to effect improvements.
3. Providing a service of information, advice, and assistance to the Suburban Store organization that will result in the maximum volume of sales being maintained consistent with the Hutzler reputation for quality and service (and in employee's restaurants consistent with Hutzler personnel standards).

Credit for the merchandising success of the Suburban Store Food Departments will be given to Manager of Food Departments.

Line and Staff Responsibilities of Downtown Store General Operating and Financial Manager's Division for Suburban Store Operation

Line Responsibilities

1. The dollar control of all assets.
2. The provision of uniform accounting and control systems, procedures, and forms.
3. Reports and statistical services.
4. The extension of credit and credit authorization.
5. The movement of merchandise to and from the Suburban Stores.

Staff Responsibilities

1. A continuing review and analysis of the Suburban Store performance of functions for which Controller is responsible Downtown.

2. Recommending action to effect improvements.
3. Providing a service of accounting and control information, advice, and assistance.

Line and Staff Responsibilities of Downtown Store Publicity Division for Suburban Store Operation

Line Responsibilities

1. Publicity and advertising for the Suburban Store.
2. Supplying advertising proofs.
3. Purchasing and supplying give-aways.
4. Fashion Shows.
5. Processing donation requests.
6. Creating, purchasing, assembling, and supplying of major and seasonal displays.
7. The installation of seasonal displays.
8. The purchasing and supply of minor displays.
9. The technical supervision of the Suburban Store Display operation.
10. Supplying all store and merchandise signs.

Staff Responsibilities

1. A continuing review and analysis of the appearance of the Suburban Store and the performance of the Suburban Store Display Department.
2. Recommend action to effect improvements.
3. Providing a service of advertising and publicity information, advice, and assistance.

Line and Staff Responsibilties of the Downtown Store General Merchandise Managers' Divisions for Suburban Store Operation

Line Responsibilities

1. The merchandise planning.
2. The purchasing and allocation of merchandise.
3. The prompt handling and filling of merchandise requisitions.
4. Seeing that Suburban Store merchandise stocks are active and well balanced.

5. The prompt review and return of Suburban Store Want Slips with action taken noted.
6. The requisitioning of all merchandise signs except replacement of signs.
7. Providing copies of all advertising copy requests and refusals to the Suburban Store.

Staff Responsibilities

1. A continuing review and analysis of the performance of the Suburban Store merchandising operation.
2. Recommending action to effect improvements.
3. Providing a service of information, advice, and assistance to the Suburban Store Organization that will result in the maximum volume of sales being maintained.

In general, the Executives of the Merchandise Division are responsible for the merchandising results of their respective departments and divisions in the Suburban Store. Credit for the merchandising success of their departments and divisions will be given to these Executives.

APPENDIX D

THE BRANCH MANAGER'S BOOKSHELF

In addition to the advice and information available to him through the main store's corps of experts, the branch manager often has occasion to consult reference works—to refresh his memory, to help train executives working under him, to make sure that no stone has been left unturned in seeking answers to specific problems.

From the list of NRMA publications, therefore, a selection has been made of those most likely to be useful to branch managers. These are shown here, with their number and member's price, for convenience in ordering. (Non-members pay higher prices.)

It should be pointed out that the National Retail Merchants Association has a staff of experts and a vast store of information always available to executives of member stores. Either directly or through his parent store, the branch manager of a member retail firm is always welcome to consult NRMA by mail, telephone, or personal visit. Headquarters are at 100 West 31st Street, New York, N.Y. 10001. The telephone is (Area 212) 244 8780.

NRMA Publications

M400—The Buyer's Manual, $5.00
SM822—Housekeeping Manual for Retail Stores, $7.50
P577—Communications—Downward and Upward, $4.50
C128—Successful Cost Cutting, $6.50
SM823—Cutting Store Expense, $4.50
SM825—400 Ways to Reduce Expense, $6.50
B98—Leased Departments (Reprinted from STORES Magazine),
25 cents
CR310—Credit in the Branch Store, $3.00
P576—Programmed Instruction for Better Training, $4.00

P561—Shoe Sales Training Manual, $3.50

Additional publications are issued each year by NRMA, to meet the growing and changing needs of retailers. To keep abreast of new publications, the branch manager should ask, directly or through his store, for a copy of the current list once or twice each year. The most recent list contains more than 150 titles.

NRMA Periodicals

To keep retailers informed of current thinking, methods, and experience, NRMA publishes a number of periodicals. Some are designed for top management; others for individual specialists within a store. A complete listing is embodied in NRMA's list of publications, mentioned above.

For the branch manager, these periodicals are particularly suggested:
B99—Stores Magazine, monthly, $8.00
SM800—Store Manager's News Bulletin, quarterly, $4.00
P504—Personnel Service, bi-monthly, $5.00
S608—The Promotion Exchange, monthly, $6.00
(Prices are those for members within the United States and Canada.)

Other Periodicals

Among the many periodicals to which retail executives subscribe, those listed below suggest themselves as supplying ideas of special value to the branch manager and his staff—product news, display ideas, sales training material, success stories of retail promotions, for example.

Before subscribing to any of these, however, the branch manager should first check with his parent store, to see if a pass-along copy is available from someone who is already subscribing. He should also check with the publication office on the price. Some publications give group rates; others supply complimentary copies; others have special rates for two-year or longer subscriptions. Prices change, too. Those shown are recent prices for single-year subscriptions, within U.S.A.

Clothes Magazine, 47 East 44 Street, New York, N.Y. 10017,
$10.00, twice a month.

Corset and Underwear Reveiew, 285 Madison Avenue, New York, N.Y. 10017, $2.00, monthly.

Daily News Record, 7 East 12 Street, New York, N.Y. 10003,
$24.00, five days a week. Textiles, men's wear.

Display World, 407 Gilbert Avenue, Cincinnati, Ohio 45202,
$7.00, monthly.

Earnshaw's, 101 West 31 Street, New York, N.Y. 10001,
$3.00, monthly. Infants', children's wear.

Footwear News, 7 East 12 Street, New York, N.Y. 10003,
$7.00, weekly.

Home Furnishings Daily, 7 East 12 Street, New York, N.Y. 10003,
$12.00, five days a week.

Housewares Review, 285 Madison Avenue, New York, N.Y. 10017,
$2.00, monthly.

Intimate Apparel, 285 Madison Avenue, New York, N.Y. 10017,
$2.00, six times a year.

Men's Wear, 7 East 12 Street, New York, N.Y. 10003,
$5.00, twice a month.

Retail Sales and Visual Promotions (R.S.V.P.), JEMS Publications,
887 Woodside Drive, Wantagh, N.Y., $6.50 monthly.

Small World, 101 West 31 Street, New York, N.Y. 10001,
$2.00, monthly. Juvenile furniture, toys, etc.

The Teens' & Boys' Outfitter, 71 West 35 Street, New York, N.Y. 10001,
$10.00, monthly.

Women's Wear Daily, 7 East 12 Street, New York, N.Y. 10003,
$24.00, five times a week.

This list is by no means exhaustive, but it serves to indicate the
variety of help available via the printed word. Discussion with the
buyer or other appropriate executive at the parent store will elicit
many additional suggestions.

Scholarly journals have not been listed, since the primary emphasis
here is on those publications that offer practical, quickly assimilated
information that the branch manager and his staff can utilize at once
and on their own.